D0502115

THE
HEART
OF
PRAISE

jack w. hayford

Regal

From Gospel Light
Ventura, California, U.S.A.

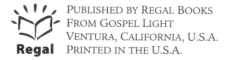

PUBLISHED BY REGAL BOOKS
FROM GOSPEL LIGHT
VENTURA, CALIFORNIA, U.S.A.
PRINTED IN THE U.S.A.

Regal Books is a ministry of Gospel Light, a Christian publisher dedicated to serving the local church. We believe God's vision for Gospel Light is to provide church leaders with biblical, user-friendly materials that will help them evangelize, disciple and minister to children, youth and families.

It is our prayer that this Regal book will help you discover biblical truth for your own life and help you meet the needs of others. May God richly bless you.

For a free catalog of resources from Regal Books/Gospel Light, please call your Christian supplier or contact us at 1-800-4-GOSPEL or www.regalbooks.com.

Library of Congress Cataloging-in-Publication Data
Hayford, Jack W.
  The heart of praise / Jack Hayford.
    p. cm.
  ISBN 0-8307-3785-5 (gift hard cover)
  1. Bible. O.T. Psalms—Meditations. 2. Devotional calendars. I. Title.
  BS1430.54.H39 2005
  242'.2—dc22   2005017335

1   2   3   4   5   6   7   8   9   10   /   10   09   08   07   06   05

Rights for publishing this book in other languages are contracted by Gospel Light Worldwide, the international nonprofit ministry of Gospel Light. Gospel Light Worldwide also provides publishing and technical assistance to international publishers dedicated to producing Sunday School and Vacation Bible School curricula and books in the languages of the world. For additional information, visit www.gospellightworldwide.org; write to Gospel Light Worldwide, P.O. Box 3875, Ventura, CA 93006; or send an e-mail to info@gospellightworldwide.org.

contents

introduction

Dear friend, I am hopeful—no, I am persuaded!—that the praise and worship you offer our heavenly Father through the Psalms in this little book can bless you beyond anything you might expect. Of course, He deserves our praise; but He also delights in it—and for a wonderful reason. He calls for our praise not because He needs a "build-up," but because the atmosphere of praise provides Him with a mighty opportunity to bless us! *God wants to bless you through worship.*

There is nothing egocentric about worshiping with that awareness in our minds. It's not a matter of our cheapening worship, seeking only to win a blessing. It's simply that our being blessed has been built in to worship as an inherent by-product in the practice of praise. God has ordained that praise and worship ascend like arrows, puncturing the heavens and allowing His abundant riches to rain down.

A word of caution: Praising God through the Psalms will change you. Although the change will be a glorious one, change is threatening to some, so I wanted to warn you. The fact is, worship *changes us into the likeness of the One we worship.*

In speaking of the worship of idols, the psalmist said, "Those who make them are like them; so is everyone who trusts in them" (Ps. 115:8). Worship has the awesome power to transform the worshiper into the image of the one worshiped. If you or I worship the god of mammon or materialism, we will become more materialistic—more ruled by the world's mind-set. Similarly, worshiping the god of unbridled sensuality has reduced many a devotee of the flesh to a fleshly degenerate. In contrast, worshiping the true and living God "in the beauty of holiness" (Ps. 29:2) will in turn make you and me more "beautiful" people—truly! Praising the God of grace will make us more gracious. We'll prove the truth of the saying, "As He is, so are we in this world" (1 John 4:17).

There is no greater pathway to praise than the Psalms. With this ancient Jewish hymnbook as the basis for our praise, we *breathe in* God's own Word while *breathing out* our worship of Him. The Psalms fairly burst with praise and adoration that glorify God for who He is, while at the same time showing us who we are. In the Psalms, we are reminded that worship is a way of telling us something about ourselves, not a ritual by which we remind God of how great He is, as though He has a low self-image and needs us to encourage Him to think better of Himself. We can learn truths about ourselves while standing with hands upraised or kneeling or lying prostrate before the Throne that we would be unable to learn in any other position.

Because so many of the Psalms were written by David, this book will also expose you to the very soul of a man who was "after [God's] own heart" (1 Sam. 13:14). In the Psalms, David and other inspired writers bring us to the heart of the kind of worship God wants. And the heart of that worship declares "worth-ship"—

God's worth and wonder. Both in his joy and in his pain, David declares God's worthiness; he reminds us that praise and worship belong both in our moments of triumph and exultation and in our experiences of life's painful extremities. As someone has said, "Faith can be born in a cry."

The guidelines for praise that follow have been arranged topically for convenient, private use in your daily devotions, or for special times of fellowship with your family or other fellow believers. For the Psalms not only lend themselves to individual worship, but they also highlight the importance of "not forsaking the assembling of ourselves together" (Heb. 10:25).

As you allow me to share my thoughts with you, I believe you'll profit from the excellent work Ron Durham has done in providing stimulating, thought-provoking questions, designed to help you apply, in practical ways, the truths I've shared. The added Scripture references are his selections, and sI thank him for his devoted work in outlining this whole project. (Incidentally, there are also some suggestions in the Appendix you might find helpful for structuring your private times of prayer and praise.)

So open your heart with me. Let's both come to Him in worship! Worship is *the* pathway, the grand entry gate, for welcoming the King of heaven into our daily lives, our families, our churches, our cities, our nation. May your use of these reflections make a straight path for His feet . . . and for yours.

Jack Hayford

The call to worship

Oh come, let us worship and bow down; let us kneel before the LORD our Maker. For He is our God, and we are the people of His pasture, and the sheep of His hand.

PSALM 95:6-7

I confess to being old enough to remember the then-famous DON MCNEIL "BREAKFAST CLUB" on radio. The program came out of Chicago and was something of the equivalent of television's more recent *Today Show*. Though I was only a boy, how well I recall how during each day's program there would be a time when Don McNeil would say, "It's prayer time around the breakfast table." Soft organ music would rise in the background, and then Don would continue, "And now, each in his own words, each in his own way, bow your heads and let us pray." It is moving to recollect such a thing being included on a secular nationwide program.

And yet there was something about Don's invitation to worship that was much more American than it was scriptural. We have a national disposition to emphasize our right to worship *in our own way*. While I'm grateful for that freedom, of course, it misses an essential fact about true worship: Biblical worship is on *God's* terms, not ours. Psalm 95, in calling us to worship, says nothing about our rights. Instead, it summarily calls us to *bow down*, to *kneel* before this One whose creatures we are—the sheep of His pasture. And make no mistake, the call to bowing and kneeling refers to more than mere bodily posture.

It focuses the surrender of our will and way to Him. It means that we are granting supreme authority to God; that in worship and in life we are giving up our will in favor of His. It notes a foundational fact about true worship: Once I choose the living God as my God, *I give up the right to worship in my own way*. In the very act of naming God "God," you and I are granting to Him alone the right to prescribe how He wishes to be worshiped.

For example, in Genesis 22, when God told Abraham to go to the land of Moriah *to worship*, we're introduced to God's ways in appointing the "worship program" for those He plans to grow up in faith's ways. Abraham had no occasion to say, "Sure, God! I will worship You—but how about in my own way, OK?" Rather, when Abraham heard God tell him that he was to worship by offering his son Isaac on an altar of sacrifice, he knew that he had to choose between his way and God's way.

What a shock to have heard God's appointed worship plan! Offer Isaac?! Not only did this act apparently go against God's revealed displeasure with pagan practices of human sacrifice, but God had actually given Isaac as a special gift to Abraham and Sarah after they were past the normal age of childbearing. And now, to demand Isaac's life? Outlandish though it seems, Abraham was ready to obey, and he told his servants something very significant: "I and the lad will go yonder and *worship*" (Gen. 22:5, *KJV,* emphasis added).

Of course, today we know the story's end: God provided another sacrifice—a ram caught in the thicket—and spared Isaac's life. Yet the New Testament says that Abraham really "offered" Isaac, because faith's living worship was found in his obedience and willingness (see Heb. 11:17). He demonstrated the basic meaning of worship: *totally giving over our human will to the will of God.*

As we begin, we are wise to expect to be *shaped* in understanding and practice as we answer God's call to worship. We'll find it not only a privilege but also a challenge. Be aware and be prepared: To grow in praise and worship is to discover new dimensions of saying to God, *Not my will but Thine be done.*

praise in prayer

O God, I confess both the difficulty and yet the desirability of totally submitting my will to Yours. Help me as I launch forward toward new, heart-felt praise and worship. And help me to love and trust You so deeply that I am assured that whatever I give up for You will be only gain for me. In the name of Jesus, amen.

selected Readings

Exodus 35:20-29   Hebrews 5:5-9

praise in practice

1. What idols or objects of worship do you find substituted for God today? Is pride often involved in the naming of these "gods"?

2. To bring this question closer to home, take a piece of paper, and on it draw a circle three or four inches in diameter.

Write inside the circle the three or four things most dear to you besides God and Christ (for example, family, work and friends). Now imagine that God calls you to sacrifice everything in the circle, leaving the circle only for Him. What would be the hardest to put outside the circle? Would you be angry with God for requiring this? Of course God does not require you to sacrifice your family. But this exercise confronts us with the *attitude* required of true worshipers.

Discoveries of praise

*Teach me Your way, O LORD; I will walk in
Your truth; unite my heart to fear Your name.
I will praise You, O Lord my God, with all my heart,
and I will glorify Your name forevermore.*

PSALM 86:11-12

people who would truly worship God must
become *teachable* people. Here, the psalmist looks
up to God with complete openness, ready both to learn
and to walk in the truth. To unfold this theme, return to
the account of Abraham's offering of Isaac. No passage in
Scripture provides more fundamental teaching on the
true meaning of worship. By being open to God's call,
Abraham discovered *a new place of worship.* "Go to the land
of Moriah," God told him, "and offer [Isaac] there as a
burnt offering on one of the mountains of which I shall
tell you" (Gen. 22:2). Abraham left the security of his car-
avan and his servants to go discover this new place—this
new mountain of acceptable worship to God.

Sometimes we must go to a new "place" too, in
order to discover the true meaning of worship. It will
probably be to a new place in our hearts or attitudes
rather than to a new physical site, but we sometimes
need to be guided away from the worn valleys of our
familiar ways to a mountain of God's assignment.
We can become so accustomed to tradition, to the
same trappings of worship and the same forms, that
the spirit of worship dies of familiarity. But let's
open as the psalmist does: "Teach me *Your* way." Let's
not fear discovering a new place of worship, where in
finding new and fresh capacities for worship, we find

new dimensions of God's goodness and Person.

Abraham first discovered that *surrendering to God's claim* is at the core of worship. Abraham thought Isaac was *his*, momentarily forgetting that Isaac was God's gift and thereby rightfully His to claim. And so it is with all of our own gifts. Everything we have has been "bought at a price" (1 Cor. 6:20), and you and I need to retain a readiness to return our "beloved Isaacs" at the center of our hearts—those things we cherish most dearly. Ever and always they must be kept before the Lord, to be sacrificed for His purpose. In the text for this reading, the psalmist promises to praise God with his whole heart, clearly meaning that nothing can be withheld. Can we begin to sense here the radical nature of true worship? It transforms our values from the beginning.

But further, Abraham discovered *the true nature of God*. He learned that God does not demand those things dearest to us because *He needs them*, but because He knows *we need* to be released from their controlling us. God never demands a sacrifice for the divine pleasure of smelling its aroma or because He needs us to tickle His pride. The objective is our release—our growth. God asked Abraham to offer Isaac neither to exploit Abraham's emotions nor to destroy Isaac's body. But what He did do was to forever take away Abraham's fear that God might not have his best interests at heart. It is only in living worship that we will draw close enough to discern God's true nature and loving heart toward us.

Abraham also discovered *the rewards of worship*. Of course, God gave Abraham no immediate monetary reward for worshiping Him, but the reward was immensely grander—*God Himself!* "I am your . . . exceedingly great reward" (Gen. 15:1). Until every corner of Abraham's heart was possessed by a trust in the greater love of God, God would be restricted from fully giving of Himself to Abraham. If he had been withholding anything from God, there wouldn't have been room in Abraham's heart to contain the wealth awaiting him in God. It's another way of saying, "No one can serve two masters" (Matt. 6:24). The sacrifice of worship establishes our servanthood to the true God.

We see then that worship has a "cutting edge"— one that cuts the flesh and prunes our preferences. Bowing before the Sovereign Lord introduces real demands but also opens new dimensions of promise. We begin to catch a glimpse of what we can discover about God and about ourselves when we are willing to be taught in worship by Him *whom* we worship.

praise in prayer

*Dear Lord, the extent of Your lordship over my life
would be frightening if I did not trust You to have
my best interests in mind. Grant me a teachable
spirit, that I may discover the riches You have in
store for those who put You first in their lives.
Through Christ I pray, amen.*

selected readings

Genesis 22:1-19   Luke 18:18-30

praise in practice

1. After giving careful thought to your pil-
   grimage in Christ, think of something
   you have learned that may never have been
   revealed to you without your first having
   accepted some discipline as a disciple of
   our Lord Jesus!
2. Do new worship forms, or even unfamil-
   iar places of worship, make you uncomfortable? Why or why not?

worship and the meaning of life

*All our days have passed away in Your wrath;
we finish our years like a sigh. The days of our lives are
seventy years; and if by reason of strength they are eighty
years, yet their boast is only labor and sorrow; for it is soon
cut off, and we fly away. So teach us to number our days,
that we may gain a heart of wisdom.*

PSALM 90:9-10,12

we are only faithful to the book of psalms when we consider its balance. It's a praise book for all seasons: For when we rejoice in the Lord and exult over His providential care and when our souls nearly burst with pain in times of darkness.

What can we do when life seems hard, defeating, unfulfilling and aimless? Well, we can be honest in our prayers, as the psalmist was. We can cry to God, echoing Psalm 90:13: "Return, O LORD! How long? And have compassion on Your servants."

Can you see what is happening here? This writer isn't crying out in dark unbelief but in the light of hope. In short, he is *worshiping*. The fact that his heart isn't overflowing with blessing or abundance is no hindrance to his worship. For this believer, his situation becomes all the more reason to seek solace and refuge in God. We would never find this believer staying home from the praise assembly muttering, "I don't feel like worshiping,"

The psalmist was wise enough to know that, as Bible translator J. B. Phillips put it, there's "a God-shaped hole that only He can fill." Or as Augustine said, "You have made us for Yourself, and our hearts find no rest until they find it in You."

Even in the dark times, we must realize the vast power of worship to give our lives meaning and purpose. For one thing, bowing before any god *declares our values.* If we surrender to the lying deity veiled in feelings of despair and aimlessness when it visits us, we bow before hopelessness, exchanging the almighty God for a lesser god. But worshiping God even amidst despair is a way to defy our adversary and declare how we value the good—the best—in life: the Lord! There is no more worthy purpose to praise and no more worthy time for it!

In worship, we also *name priorities.* Putting God first enables us to focus on first things—His love, our blessings, our responsibilities to others—instead of the temporary feelings of despair. Worship sets the priority of the One to whom we look for guidance. It even forms certain expectations, so that our worship determines what we will yet discover in our future.

Worship is also a way of *setting goals,* removing the sense that we're not going anywhere. Just the act of acknowledging that *God,* not the darkness, holds our future can enable us to "number our days"—to entrust our way to Him even when it's too dark to see our next step.

The despairing moment in which the psalmist wrote this text eventually passed. He overcame by insisting on remaining in God's presence, even when the Temple was dark and he could not see the way. Just so, in our own times of confusion and aimlessness, when we remember the power of worshiping in the darkness, we will be able to order our days aright and to finish them not with a sigh, but with a joyous shout!

praise in prayer

Dear Lord, as I come before You, I confess that without You, life is meaningless. Grant me, as I praise You, a vision of who I am and what I am to do. Help me to order my days in ways that glorify Your name. Even when I cannot see my way, help me to trust Your providence. Through Jesus, my Lord, amen.

selected readings

Psalm 90:11-17   Ecclesiastes 12:1-7,13

praise in practice

1. In what specific ways does your faith give meaning and purpose to your life? It may be helpful to group your answers in the categories this devotional suggests: (1) values, (2) priorities, and (3) aims, or goals.
2. The book of Ecclesiastes is even more skeptical about life's meaning and purpose than Psalm 90 is. But a recurring phrase in the book specifies the limited viewpoint to which its skepticism applies. What is that limited arena? (See the last phrase in Ecclesiastes 1:3 and 2:11.)

The Beauty of Holiness

Give unto the LORD, O you mighty ones,
give unto the LORD glory and strength. Give unto the
LORD the glory due to His name; worship the
LORD in the beauty of holiness.

PSALM 29:1-2

All of us have our own ideas about what makes a worship service beautiful. The fact that we sometimes disagree on this issue may indicate that we are missing a clue the psalmist gives here about worship's intent. The text points to something called "the beauty of holiness." It seems that through worship, God wants to meet us and pour *His* beauty and holiness into our lives. Could it be that if our worship more frequently "beautified" us, we would more readily find "holiness" than we do through self-constructed programs of religious effort?

This psalm's mention of the presence of the holy God may seem threatening to some, prompting them to recoil in feelings of unworthiness or self-disgust rather than being attracted to God's holiness. How many of us feel all too keenly that, in comparison to the all-holy One, we are anything but holy?! That was the prophet Isaiah's experience when he saw a vision of the Lord "high and lifted up" (Isa. 6:1), with the seraphim—those mysterious creatures that surround God's throne—who ceaselessly worship God's holiness, crying, "Holy, holy, holy is the LORD of hosts; the whole earth is full of His glory!" (Isa. 6:3).

Isaiah could only cry out, "Woe is me!" (Isa. 6:5) Interestingly, we can almost hear a good Jewish worshiper like Isaiah call out, *"Oveh!"*—that's the Hebrew word used here for "woe." Then the prophet adds, "For I am undone! Because I am a man of unclean lips, and I dwell in the midst of a people of unclean lips; for my eyes have seen the King, the LORD of hosts" (6:5).

Surely our own worship would be shallow if we could not feel, as Isaiah did, something of the fearful distance between God's holiness and ours. Yet there is more to worship than this! Suddenly one of the seraphim flies to the altar of sacrifice, takes a coal from it, touches the prophet's tongue with the burning coal and says, "Behold, this has touched your lips; your iniquity is taken away, and your sin purged" (Isa. 6:7).

From one standpoint, we are exactly right if we feel that we're too sinful to stand in the presence of God and worship. But we need to let our worship "in Christ"—in "the beauty of *His* holiness"—remind us how His cleansing blood has touched us. Not only our tongues but also our whole being has been washed in the blood of the Lamb (see Rev. 7:14)! It *is* overwhelming to reflect on our sinfulness before a sinless God; but let us recognize with equal impact that through Christ we have been cleansed, enabled through His righteousness to stand before the holy God.

If we dare to confess that we have been stained with sin, we can also believe with equal boldness that Christ's holiness will clothe us. In the beauty of holiness—in robes of righteousness—He enables us to stand before Him, high and lifted up though He is, and our worship is fully accepted by Him! As we worship, let us welcome the fire of God's altar applied directly to any failure of ours that remains. As Isaiah's "unclean lips" troubled him, and were purged, believe that whatever troubles you have may be similarly purged as you worship, thereby discovering *more* of "the beauty of holiness" as it overwhelms our unholiness!

praise in prayer

Holy, holy, holy, Lord God Almighty! Through the blood of Christ, I praise You for clothing me in His righteousness and admitting me into Your Throne Room to gaze on the beauty of Your holiness. Amen.

selected readings

Isaiah 6:1-8   Revelation 4:6-11

praise in practice

1. Picture or describe the most beautiful worship setting you've ever seen. Was it in a cathedral? A woodland setting? A view from a mountaintop? Now compare that scene with the awesome picture painted in Isaiah 6:1-8. Dwell on that until the beauty of the other scenes fade in comparison with the beauty of God's own holiness.

2. Practice—now and several times throughout the next day or two—this twofold prayer of *confession* and *consolation*: (1) ask God to forgive your sins in the name of Christ, then (2) affirm joyfully, *"My sins are forgiven!"* Do you find it harder to affirm forgiveness than to confess sin? If so, how might this inhibit your worship?

pain and praise and the presence of God

O My God, I cry in the daytime, but You do not hear; and in the night season, and am not silent. But You are holy, enthroned in the praises of Israel.

PSALM 22:2-3

The psalms, though they are great, swelling songs to God, can often be raw and ragged because they are so honest to life as well as honest to God. They give vent to sorrow and anguish as well as to exultation. Some people mistakenly think that life has to go smoothly in order for them to worship. Not the psalmists. To be sure, the psalmists can shout and sing with joy, but they also know to worship when the heart is burdened with grief. And sometimes their songs are wrenched from their groanings.

The psalmists reveal that worship is appropriate in every setting and circumstance of life and that you and I can develop a capacity for praise that will allow it to break through to God quite independently of any night seasons we may be going through.

Once, when my schedule had weighed me down with an awful burden of mental and spiritual pressure, I took a break and traveled up Highway 1, which curves along California's beautiful Pacific coastline. When I came to a little spot called Jade Cove, I stopped the car and walked down to the edge of the ocean. I heard the crashing of the waves and felt their spray on my face. And there, semisurrounded by the splashing sea, I poured out my plight in prayer, just as

David had done in Psalm 22.

Suddenly, with an inexplicable lifting effect, a marvelous flood of peace swept over me. It seemed almost as though Jesus had walked across the surf to be with me, just as He had walked on the waters of Galilee to be with His disciples (see John 6:17-21). In that moment, He was *present* there *with me,* and the ministering might of His presence lifted my burden and powerfully transformed my world—lifting the load of fear and pressure from my mind.

God had honored His promise through David to inhabit the praises of His people. Here, the Hebrew word for "inhabit" is translated "enthroned," opening the passage to show us its meaning: *God creates a dwelling place among those who praise Him.* It doesn't specify whether the worshiper needs be hurting or joy-filled at the moment, but it's moving to note the text as one in which the praiser is at a point of despair.

Here is a magnificent truth! Just as God is sovereign whether we worship Him or not, He will indwell us mightily and majestically *when we praise Him,* whether we are feeling happy or sad. Praise constructs a throne room in our hearts where the Sovereign God declares that He is pleased to dwell.

Despite any burden or pressure you may be feeling at this moment, let me encourage you to open your heart and worship Him who invites you to "come to Me, all you who labor and are heavy laden, and I will give you rest" (Matt. 11:28). When you answer with worship, the miracle will occur, for it is in worship that you and I will discover anew that "the tabernacle of God is with men" (Rev. 21:3).

praise in prayer

God enthroned above, I praise You for also dwelling in my heart. You know what makes me weep even before I do. Lift my vision above my burdens and enable me to live in the power of praise. Through Christ our Lord, amen.

selected readings

Psalm 103:1-18   John 14:1-6

praise in practice

1. Imagine that you are bringing a problem wrapped in what I call a "burden bundle" to the throne of Jesus. Picture Him reaching out and offering to take the bundle. Does the picture include your being all too glad to turn it over to Him, or do you imagine yourself hesitating? Are you aware of any reluctance? Do you fear what might be required of you if you let Him bear the burden? Remember that *trust* is a part of praise.

2. Recall the burden that Christ bore on the cross—the sins of the world. Compare any burdens that you may have just now with that burden. This isn't to say that your own burden is trivial, but to help put your life in perspective as you view it from the Cross.

3. Set aside some time—just 5 to 10 minutes each day—in which you can think quietly about only the praise points, or blessings, in your life. You may want to include reflecting on the Psalms as part of these quiet times.

All you need is a broken heart

For You do not desire sacrifice, or else I would give it;
You do not delight in burnt offering. The sacrifices of God
are a broken spirit, a broken and a contrite heart.

PSALM 51:16-17

I love laughter and song and just plain joyfulness as much as anyone. Yet there is a forced happiness among some church folk that makes me uncomfortable. You know the line—"You just lost your job? Well, praise God for that, brother!" Or, "My mother is dying of cancer, but I'm still just praising the Lord."

Not only can this kind of response be a study in religiously generated dishonesty, but it can also cause those who overhear such talk think that if they can't bring themselves to make such glib affirmations, they're in no position—or disposition—to worship or exercise the power of faith. The truth is, true worship may *result* in happiness or bright emotions, but it is also subject to the entire range of human emotion, including the broken heart David describes (see Ps. 51:17).

In one sense, brokenness is the very essence of worship. It was physically required when animals were slain in Old Testament worship, for the "perfect" sacrifices were "broken" when slain. They were not only a substitute atonement for the sin of the worshiper, but they were also a sacrifice of self. The gift of life indicated that the worshiper was giving up his own interests, sacrificing his ownership of an animal in honor of the superior "worth-ship" of God. That's why the animal could not be crippled or blemished, for such an offering, being "worth-less," would reflect on the worthiness of God and demonstrate a less than sincere or full understanding on the part of the worshiper (see Lev. 1:2-3).

Unfortunately, the fact that these sacrifices were costly led some to think that the more expensive the gift, the more God would be pleased, and thus, the greater would be the blessing bestowed upon the worshiper. But God was interested in the worshiper's heartfelt *obedience*—in the attitude of heart represented by the *offering*—not solely in who could afford to bring the most oxen or sheep to the altar. This, of course, is what led David to affirm the beautiful truth of Psalm 51: "The sacrifices of God are a broken spirit, a broken and a contrite heart—these, O God, You will not despise."

The story surrounding the text dramatically emphasizes this truth. Remember the depth of David's sin, his adultery with Bathsheba and his gross attempt to cover it up with her husbands, Uriah's, murder? As a wealthy king, David could have afforded to offer thousands of oxen or sheep or goats, but there weren't enough animals in the world to compensate for his sin. No altar could have been built large enough to receive enough animal sacrifices. It was David's *heart* that had been closed to the will of God and had sinned so willfully. But now, opening his will to heartfelt repentance, King David humbly asked for a new capacity to praise: "O Lord, open my lips, and my mouth shall show forth Your praise" (Isa. 51:15).

This was when David received the remarkable revelation of the sacrifice God really wants from each of us: All we need is a broken heart! Ultimately, it was not the sight of an animal sacrifice that moved God to grant forgiveness and to receive David back into His embrace. It was David's broken heart—the spirit that had grown tender enough to be pained by sin.

There's no need to be embarrassed if you can't bring to God a jolly heart every time you feel the need to praise Him. There's no shame in not being able to afford an expensive gift, as though you could buy God off and purchase forgiveness. Just bring Him your heart, broken though it may be. That's what He has wanted from you all along.

praise in prayer

O God, I give You my heart, for You are Lord of my life. Even when I am sorrowful—even when I am less than I want to be—I praise You as a God who accepts the open and honest heart over any material sacrifice I could bring. In the name of Christ, my Savior, amen.

selected readings

Psalm 51:10-19   Luke 18:9-14

praise in practice

1. In your own experience, are people more likely to praise God when they are feeling up or when they are painfully aware of their shortcomings?

2. The psalmist said in Psalm 77:3, "I remembered God, and was troubled." Some people find it surprising to learn that thinking about God doesn't always produce a happy heart. Read this verse in context (Psalm 77:1-9) and think about the reasons for the psalmist's sadness. Was his mood appropriate?

3. Notice also that the psalmist doesn't stay in such depression. Read verses 10-15 and describe the specific steps the psalmist took to move from sorrow to praise.

DAY 7

on not being lonely even when alone

A father of the fatherless, a defender of widows,
is God in His holy habitation. God sets the solitary
in families; He brings out those who are
bound into prosperity.

PSALM 68:5-6

Those who live alone—single adults, those who have lost a beloved family member, widows and widowers, people who have simply been abandoned—can sometimes feel so isolated, estranged and lonely that it's easy for them to feel abandoned by God as well. In Psalm 68:5-6, the psalmist calls us to worship the One who personally knows and loves us. We are shown how God wants to help us see that He delights to "[set] the solitary in families" (Ps. 68:6) through healthy Christian fellowship.

Once as I was struggling through the genealogy in the first chapter of Matthew, I found myself thinking, *What an uninteresting way to begin the New Testament—with lists and lists of names.* But as I paused to inquire of the Lord, praying for insight, it occurred to me that God put such lists of names in the Bible for at least three reasons: (1) He cares about and remembers individual people and calls them by name; (2) He makes promises to people and keeps those promises; and (3) He accomplishes His purpose in imperfect and fallible people.

God asserts His knowing us individually, being able to see our frame in the womb even before birth, when we were "yet unformed" (see Ps. 139:15-16). It is because God *does* keep each of us specifically and personally on His mind that He knows the exact number of hairs on our head (see Matt. 10:30). If God did not literally see and know you and me, if He did not love each of us individually even when we feel isolated from Him as well as from other people, Paul wouldn't have affirmed Jesus' death as having been for him personally: "I live by faith in the Son of God, who loved *me* and gave Himself for *me*" (Gal. 2:20, emphasis added). But our text adds to this, showing how God goes even further than individual care. He works at grouping us so that loneliness can be removed from our lives.

God has set us in the family—the Church—partly because we need each other. I need you to help complete what I am to become, and you need me and several others in the fellowship who can touch your life. You see, all of us—single or "joined"—need not only to be reborn, but also to be *rebuilt*. Not everyone contributes in the same way; sometimes some people may seem more of a liability than an asset to your building program. But the Word of God reminds us that "none of us lives to himself, and no one dies to himself" (Rom. 14:7).

This one verse summarizes a biblical principle that is far more than a mere social commentary regarding mutual goodwill. It is a conclusive statement from the Holy Spirit, teaching us that our lives are irrevocably integrated in the affairs of others. If we try to avoid learning what God wants to do in us through those relationships, we withdraw at our own expense, and we'll be poorer for having done so.

After saying this, we should also acknowledge that not everyone who is alone is lonely. As it is often said, one is a *whole* number. Some people have found that flying solo can bring the riches of solitude instead of the poverty of loneliness. Sometimes such people who have come to terms with themselves as whole persons are the best equipped for the interactions inherent in fellowship with others—they know better than most where the boundaries of the personality are.

Still, all of us, however capably we handle our lives, need other people. That's why God has set the solitary in His spiritual family—to help each of us nurture and rebuild each other. Our growth and healing depend on it!

praise in prayer

Dear Father, the world is so large, and even crowds can be so lonely. I need Your companionship and the love of brothers and sisters. Help me not to resist the very way that You have planned for me to grow. In the name of Jesus I pray, amen.

selected readings

Romans 15:1-7   1 Corinthians 12:12-22

praise in practice

1. Do you ever experience feelings of loneliness—whether you're single or living in a family? Do you have areas of interest, important life questions or needs that you feel as if no one else shares? Make a point to explore the possibility that others in your circle of acquaintances have similar needs. It may be that they are sim-

ply reluctant to say so.

2. If you live in a family, plan to invite one or more single people to a meal or an outing. If you live alone, plan a similar time with someone else in your spiritual family.

3. Look up the word "xenophobia" in a dictionary. What do you think causes xenophobia? What might cure it?

HOW TO KNOW
God's will for
your life

The secret of the LORD is with those who fear Him,
and He will show them His covenant.

PSALM 25:14

Religion is often associated with secret knowledge. Bible historians tells us about a style of thinking called gnosticism, a religious philosophy that was very prevalent in New Testament times. The word "gnostic" is from the Greek *gnosis,* meaning "knowledge." This ancient movement's appeal was that it promised that its adherents would learn secret words, see secret things, be initiated into a fellowship of secret rites. It appealed to human pride, to those who sought an elite order of relationship with the supernatural.

The psalmist holds belief to the contrary. God's secrets are not revealed to an elite but to those who fear Him—those who honor, respect and obey Him. The *New International Version* translates the verse in a more personal way: "The LORD confides in those who fear him." Imagine being the confidant of the Creator and Sustainer of the universe, in whom lie all of life's secrets! Think of being able to know the will of Him who "does great things which we cannot comprehend" (Job 37:5), knowing the One who knows "by what way is light diffused" (38:24) and "from whose womb comes the ice" (38:29).

In short, the point is that the primary part of God's master plan for the ages is an open book to those who enter into covenant with Him, for that plan is *Jesus!* You don't have to be initiated into a secret society to relate to the God of the Bible. There are no secret formulas or magic words to learn. In fact, much of the New Testament was written to combat this very kind of thinking.

Paul warns Timothy, his son in the faith, to avoid "the profane and idle babblings and contradictions of what is falsely called knowledge [gnosis]" (1 Tim. 6:20). He continues by noting that those who profess it "have strayed concerning the faith" (1 Tim. 6:21). Throughout the whole of the New Covenant Scriptures, inspired writers insist that God has revealed His whole plan for the ages through Jesus Christ: "This thing was not done in a corner" (Acts 26:26). Christian life, which is nothing less than the life of worship, is not mystical or magical. It's lived and expressed in the light, not in secret meeting places or dark, secluded caves.

God reveals His covenant to anyone who is willing to believe in His Son, trust Him enough to accept Him, and then has the humility to walk and grow in a reverent, childlike spirit—always confessing that without Him he or she doesn't know the way at all!

If you feel a hunger or desire for more specific knowledge of God's Person or His will for your life, check the depth and integrity of your worship and service—the specifics of fearing the Lord. In Romans 12:1-2, Paul tells us that this kind of wholehearted worship means that you must "present your [body as] a living sacrifice, holy, acceptable to God." And he teaches that it is in this kind of whole life commitment, not in learning supernatural secrets that have been withheld from others, "that you may prove what is that good and acceptable and perfect will of God."

praise in prayer

I praise You, O God, for revealing Your plan for the ages through Jesus Christ and for entrusting me with that revelation. Help me to discern Your voice above the clamor of life and to honor and reverence You in order to be Your close companion and confidant. Through Christ our Lord, amen.

selected readings

Job 38:1-11   1 Corinthians 2:1-10

praise in practice

1. What differences are there between wanting to know about God and actually *fearing* Him (in the biblical sense of having reverence for Him)?

2. Are there particular areas of your life for which you long to know more about God's will? If you're comfortable doing so, share these areas with other believers and invite their input.

3. What guidelines can you suggest for discerning God's specific will? How can you distinguish His voice from the voice of others or from that of your own self-interest?

4. In your daily routine, be sure to include a time for being quiet before the Lord and listening for Him to speak His will. Perhaps now is a good time and place to do this.

Let *All* That Is in Me Cry, "Holy!"

Vindicate me, O LORD, for I have walked in my integrity. I have also trusted in the LORD; I shall not slip. Examine me, O LORD, and prove me; try my mind and my heart.

PSALM 26:1-2

The concept of integrity in this psalm is interesting in connection with the praise and worship of God. Certainly David isn't claiming to be sinless, for he had already confessed his sin; rather, he rises to declare His integrity. This English word "integrity," derived from the same root as our word "integer," meaning "a whole number," expresses David's assertion that God had made him a whole person in his lifestyle and relationships. When confronted with sin, David confessed and repented. He did not want to keep any part of himself from God. All that was in him cried "Holy!"—that is, "God, let Your holy completeness fill in and fill out the broken and hollow places created by my sin and failure!"

The wisdom of New Testament worship is that it isn't just a head trip, a mystical consciousness or an emotional binge. It is our *whole* person coming before the *holy* God to be made fully holy and whole—aglow with the life of the Spirit. Paul said it plainly enough in 1 Thessalonians 5:23:

> Now may the God of peace Himself sanctify you completely [wholly, *KJV*]; . . . your whole spirit, soul, and body . . . at the coming of our Lord Jesus Christ.

Let us then worship with a *regenerated spirit,* connecting the eternal part of our beings with the Eternal Spirit of God. Let us worship with a *renewed mind,* seeking to know as fully as we can the God whom we worship. Let us praise God with *revived emotions,* not allowing pseudosophistication to make us too embarrassed for passionate praise. And let us not be afraid to worship God with a *rededicated body,* placing it, as it were, on the altar of sacrifice as well as incorporating appropriate postures in our worship.

We have all probably attended some services in which worshiping God with the physical body seemed out of place. I have no desire to put down anyone's Christian heritage—there are very understandable historical reasons for the different Christian traditions of worship. But I can't help but point out that if we ever reduce worship to a purely mental action, we're going against the grain not only of Scripture, but of what we know about human nature as well.

For years now, authorities in both physical and mental health fields have remarked on the need to integrate the whole nature of our persons in our practical life. This is but the start of what the Bible means when the word "holy" is used. "Holy" is related to "whole"—to our *whole*hearted response to God's *holy* claim on us. It is an integrating of the reality of the realm of the spirit, the realm of the physical and the realm of the mind. Holy wholeness! Whole holiness!

Let us then also acknowledge the wholesomeness and holiness of worshiping with body, soul and spirit. There's a very good reason for it: God wants *all* of you in His service—not just your head, not just your heart, but also your hands to do His bidding, your feet to run His race. He wants your entire self as a spiritual sacrifice.

praise in prayer

Dear heavenly Father, I praise You for Your whole creation, for the material as well as the spiritual world. Help me to present my whole being— thoughts, words, emotions and actions—as a living sacrifice in my worship and living. Through Jesus' love I pray, amen.

selected Readings

1 Thessalonians 5:23-24   James 1:21-27

praise in practice

1. Do you find it embarrassing to be demonstrative in worship—as in raising your hands in prayer? Why or why not? How about bowing your head? Kneeling? Think about and discuss your feelings about these ways of "worshiping with the body."

2. What parallel between worship "with the whole person" and Christian living does this chapter suggest?

3. For many people, Christianity as a merely mental matter or idea extends not only to worship but also to their concept of heaven. But what do you think the apostle Paul meant by the concept of our having a "spiritual body" in the world to come (see 1 Cor. 15:35-55)?

with my hands lifted up

*Because Your lovingkindness is better than life,
my lips shall praise You. Thus I will bless You while
I live; I will lift up my hands in Your name.*

PSALM 63:3-4

continuing our theme of worshiping God in body, soul, mind and spirit, we note here that the psalmist threw himself, lips and hands, into praising God! He illustrates the time-honored practice of extending the hands upward in worship. In the name of being modern, have we ever felt too sophisticated to do as the psalmist did? Can we not follow the apostle Paul's admonition to "pray everywhere, lifting up holy hands" (1 Tim. 2:8)?

The beautifully expressive hands of the Hawaiian dancer or the hands of the signer to the deaf are eloquent illustrations of the fact that we do not communicate merely with the tongue. Millions have marveled at the expressiveness of Albrecht Dürer's engraving *Praying Hands*, their appreciation of it sharpened when they hear that they were the hands of Dürer's brother, who earned a living doing manual labor in order that Albrecht might study art.

Hands speak volumes in Christian worship, too. The upward reach of worshiping hands is a confession that God is above us—although not in the spatial sense. (Remember the report of the first Russian cosmonaut that he hadn't seen God in space, implying that He therefore doesn't exist? The cosmonaut's conclusion is, of course, based on such a pathetic misunderstanding.) Rather, we acknowledge God's above-ness as a confession of His divine superiority. The outstretched hands turned palm outward in praise may signal our *extending* to God our praise and our love, while hands turned palm upward in worship seem to express our plea for more and more of the filling of His Holy Spirit.

Notice that the psalmist speaks of God's lovingkindness as being "better than life" (Ps. 63:3) in the same breath as his statement about worshiping with uplifted hands. It's not that he doesn't appreciate his temporal life, but in worship he reaches for more of God's dimensions of life. Remember that the gift of eternal life promised to the believer is not just life *unending*, but it is also life *unlimited*. It is life like that of the eternal God's, eternal in *quantity* but also eternal in *quality*, since He presently infuses us with the traits of His lovingkindness. That's worth reaching for!

There is something exhilarating and liberating about standing with arms upstretched in worship. Gone are the limitations of merely horizontal life, with its misunderstandings and miscommunication in human speech. For in worshipful prayer the Spirit expresses our unspeakable longings (see Rom. 8:26).

Gone are the inhibitions and intimidation we experience in most of our human interactions, for we are reaching for intimacy with God as a baby reaches for a loving parent. When we reach toward the skies, we may also confess our willingness to grow heavenward, refusing to be confined to earthbound sordidness. The openness of upstretched arms can—indeed, should—speak of all this.

praise in prayer

I reach up to You, O Father, acknowledging Your greatness, asking for more of You in my life, and putting myself in a position of growth and ever-expanding consciousness of and availability to You and Your will in my life. Through Jesus' name, amen.

selected readings

Psalm 134   Lamentations 3:37-41

praise in practice

1. If you are not a regular hand-raiser and you feel a little awkward about it, try going outdoors on a comfortable night and lifting your hands up toward the heavens. No one sees you (as though that really mattered!) and you're away from distractions and inhibitions. What does the experience make you want to say to God?

2. Let's suppose it does matter what people think. What do you think a non-Christian who is attending a Christian worship service (who is not prejudiced one way or the other) would think is signified by the congregation's upraised hands?

3. A book on worship by Robert Webber has the intriguing title *Worship Is a Verb*. What does this title imply and how might it relate to the topic of this chapter?

I will sing of the mercies of the Lord

Sing out the honor of His name; make His praise glorious. All the earth shall worship You and sing praises to You; they shall sing praises to Your name.

PSALM 66:2,4

Both Judaism and Christianity are singing faiths. There are so many references to music and singing in the Psalms that they have been called Israel's hymnbook. The word "psalm" actually means "song," originally referring to words sung to the accompaniment of a psaltery, an ancient stringed instrument. Psalm singing was important from the very beginning of Christianity, especially to express the sheer exuberance and joy that Christians experience. "Is anyone cheerful? Let him sing psalms" (Jas. 5:13).

Every period of renewal in Christian history has been accompanied by renewed interest in what believers sing. During periods of spiritual decline in the Middle Ages, monks were careful to preserve the Psalms both in writing and singing. The work of Martin Luther in this area is well known. We still drink of the streams of the Reformation when we sing Luther's great hymn, "A Mighty Fortress Is Our God." During the Reformation in Scotland, the Psalms, in rhythmic paraphrase, were a source of much of the sturdiness of Scottish faith.

We recall that King David, the author of so many of the Psalms, was a singer and harpist himself. One of the Bible's earliest portraits of David depicts him playing and singing for King Saul in order to calm the king's rages (see 1 Sam. 16:23). We can well imagine Saul's mad ravings subsiding under such reassuring lyrics as, "Whenever I am afraid, I will trust in You. . . . I will not fear. What can flesh do to me?" (Ps. 56:3-4).

Part of the power of song is that it is a beautiful expression of devotion both for the solitary worshiper in private devotions, at work or in the car, and for the congregation gathered for public worship. People can make no sound more expressive than when they sing. Singing releases the pent-up joy and thanksgiving we feel because of God's grace and goodness. For this reason the psalmist sings, "To You, O my Strength, I will sing praises" (Ps. 59:17).

Through song we can also teach and admonish each other: "Do not be drunk with wine, in which is dissipation; but be filled with the Spirit, speaking to one another in psalms and hymns and spiritual songs, singing and making melody in your heart to the Lord" (Eph. 5:18-19).

You say you don't have a good voice? You don't know how to read music? Both can be developed, but just sing anyway! Remember, God likes your voice, and even if you never learn to carry a tune, use it. You carry around with you the most important instrument for singing: *your heart*. Make melody in and with it!

praise in prayer

O Lord, our hearts sometimes feel as if they will burst with joy and thanksgiving for Your gifts and grace. Thank You for allowing us to express this in song, and thank You for those who can inspire us with music. Accept our singing, however imperfect, for the melody in our hearts, amen.

selected readings

Exodus 15:1-21   Revelation 15:1-4

praise in practice

1. If you know the following songs, or have access to them in a hymnbook, sing "I Will Sing Unto the Lord" and "Sing Hallelujah to His Name."

2. Do you think the music at the church where you worship is a good ministry to the Lord and uplifting for the worshipers? If not, what positive and constructive changes can you suggest?

3. What are some of your favorite hymns? Why do you appreciate them—because they are old favorites, because of their message, because of the mood or tone they set?

4. What do you think about contemporary Christian music, especially Christian rock music?

what language shall i borrow?

*Praise is awaiting You, O God, in Zion; and to
You the vow shall be performed. O You who
hear prayer, to You all flesh will come.*

PSALM 65:1-2

God has designed worship to fit every aspect of our nature. And as we've already noted, He wants us to employ every part of ourselves—body and soul, mind and spirit—in glorifying and worshiping Him. Let's now focus on another aspect of worshiping God with the mind—specifically, the use of human speech in praising God.

Speech is foremost among the gifts that distinguish human beings from animals. Our capacity for the most common conversation or for the most learned discourse is a result of our having been created in the image of God. It is also a key to our exercising the dominion that God has given humankind to rule over the rest of His creation (see Gen. 1:28). The responsible exercise of that rule requires sensitive and sensible communication and flows most effectively out of our daily communication offered to God in worship and prayer.

In His wisdom, God has ordained several different kinds of prayer. If we think of the act of prayer as a fruit basket filled with a variety of lovely fruits that we may bring to God as a gift, we will better grasp the admonition of Hebrews 13:15: "By Him let us continually offer the sacrifice of praise to God, that is, the fruit of our lips, giving thanks to His name." Let's sample the variety.

First, let us approach God with the language, or prayer, of *confession*, acknowledging our sins and imperfection and our longing to partake of His holiness.

Second, let us continue to offer the fruit of our lips with the language of *petition*. Here we recall that He has promised, "Ask, and it will be given to you" (Matt. 7:7). But we also petition God that we might understand what we are to do for Him, praying for insight into His will for us.

Third, with the language of *praise* He enables us to "enter into His gates with thanksgiving, and into His courts with praise" (Ps. 100:4). We remain in His presence as we worship by recalling His goodness, His love and the grandeur of His being.

Fourth, *meditation* is also a part of our speech in God's presence. This form of prayer was never meant as some mystical way of uniting with the universe, but it has been given as a way of *waiting* upon God, knowing that just being in His presence deepens our intimacy with Him.

Fifth and sixth, in prayer our speech also includes *intercession* and *supplication*. There's never a shortage of situations that need His intervention. So we intercede—being bold enough to ask Him to step into the middle of a muddle! Supplication is contracting with God to invade our present dilemma with His wisdom, power and provision.

Finally, our worshipful praying includes *exaltation* and *adoration*. We magnify Him who is worthy above all others and adore Him simply because of who He is.

Man uses the gift of speech for many purposes and in many ways. Because language is a function of the intellect, we have the choice between speaking in ways and words that glorify God or in language that dishonors Him. Prayer is the best exercise of our intelligence, which—though limited at best—is a mighty means to honor our Creator with "the fruit of our lips" (Heb. 13:15).

praise in prayer

You know my prayers, O Lord, even before I put them into words. I praise You for the gift of language. I ask only that my speech, both in worship and in everyday life, will glorify You. Through Christ Jesus my Lord, amen.

selected Readings

Psalm 32:1-7   Matthew 6:5-15

praise in practice

1. Sing one or more of your favorite prayer songs. Here are a few suggestions: "Dear Lord and Father of Mankind" (confession) and "Thou Art Worthy" (praise and exaltation).

2. What are some experiences you have had with answered prayer?

3. What about unanswered prayer? What attitude should we have about prayers that seemingly go unanswered?

4. Which of the kinds of prayers examined in this chapter does God most often hear arising from your lips?

worship and the word

Oh, that my ways were directed to keep
Your statutes! Then I would not be ashamed,
when I look into all Your commandments.
I will keep Your statutes.

PSALM 119:5-6,8

IT IS IMPOSSIBLE TO WORSHIP GOD ACCEPTABLY UNLESS WE COME TO HIM IN RIGHT RELATIONSHIP TO HIS STATUTES—THE WORD OF GOD. It is folly to suppose that we can come to Him "in the Spirit" if in our own spirits there is a tendency to neglect commitment to actually do what the Bible asks of us.

Much of the book of Hebrews compares and contrasts our relationship to God under the New Covenant with Israel's relationship to Him under the Old. Again and again, the Hebrew writer refers to God's requirement that the Tabernacle—that great Temple in the wilderness—and its appointments be patterned according to His Word through Moses. In Hebrews, there is always this sobering sense of "if it was that way then, how much more so now. . ."

Yet, however sincerely we relate to the Word of God, we seem always to do so imperfectly. None of us knows it all, nor are we able to plumb the Word's depths and come up with precisely the right understanding of every facet of its truth. So what are we to do?

The answer is to stay with the writer of Hebrews, allowing him to explain how Christ has already built the perfect tabernacle for us. "Christ came as High Priest of the good things to come, with the greater and more perfect tabernacle not made with hands. . . . Not with the blood of goats and calves, but with His own blood He entered the Most Holy Place once for all, having obtained eternal redemption" (Heb. 9:11-12).

This does not dismiss us from our responsibility to obey His Word of the New Covenant. It simply means that it is through the sufficiency of Jesus, not through our ability to know Scripture perfectly, that we are now able to stand in right relationship to His Word. Christ, in fact, creates in the genuine worshiper a spirit of willingness to follow His Word as it is revealed to him or her.

How often I have heard some people say, when first hearing or seeing God being worshiped in the Spirit as His Word calls us to do, "Well, that's just not my style." Beloved, the idea is that when you and I come to God, He transforms us—changes us—into *His* style. You did know, didn't you, that when you came to Him, transformation was what it was all about—that you can't come into the presence of the living God without being changed? We don't just "fake it" in the name of the Spirit! We *grow,* we *learn,* we are *shaped* by the power of the Word, which has been given to us by the Holy Spirit (see 2 Pet. 1:19-21).

True worship is never separate from the Word. We hear the Word of grace that comes to us as coals from the altar on which Christ gave Himself for us, burning away our misunderstandings and inadequate knowledge. Hearing that Word of forgiveness for our sin and failures not only makes us want all the more to worship and praise Him, but also to say, "Speak, Lord, Your servant is listening. Command, and I will obey."

praise in prayer

We praise You, dear Father, not just for the way worship can cause our spirits to soar, but for Your Word that tells us what our lives and our worship should be. Help us to connect with You in our understanding of the Word and in our times of praise. Through Christ our Lord, amen.

selected readings

1 Samuel 15:10-22   Hebrews 4:11-16

praise in practice

1. Do you feel any conflict between the rational task of Bible study—really digging deeply into the Word—and the emotional experience of praising and worshiping in the Spirit? Discuss the similarities and differences.

2. How can following the moral and ethical principles in the Word be occasions of praise and worship to God in our daily lives?

3. In 1 Samuel 15:10-22 (see the selected readings above), what was wrong with King Saul's attempt to offer sacrifices in worship to God?

4. How can we know that the Holy Spirit will not tell us to do anything that is in violation of Scripture?

Aggressiveness
in worship

*Let the saints be joyful in glory; let them sing aloud
on their beds. Let the high praises of God be in their mouth,
and a two-edged sword in their hand.*

PSALM 149:5-6

in calling us to worship, God is up to far more than cultivating a band of humble worshipers; He is building an army of triumphant warriors. This is why Psalm 149 speaks of "the high praises of God" in the same breath as "a two-edged sword." Of course, we are dealing here not with weapons of carnal warfare, but with putting our words into action by boldly going on the offensive of faith—by *acting* on the promises of the God we praise.

Let us turn to the dramatic scene in 2 Chronicles 20. King Jehoshaphat, undermanned and relatively powerless, has been brought word that "a great multitude is coming against you" (20:2). Listen to it, fellow servant! You know (or know someone who knows) that empty feeling: Word comes of a dreaded terminal disease; an accountant's report says the business is going under; a loved one tells you that your relationship is about to be broken in divorce or abandonment. This text gives direction on what can be done in such moments; something besides resigning to a passive prayer for strength. There are four action steps—four ways to take up the sword of worship.

First, the king proclaimed a *fast* (see 2 Chron. 20:3). Is fasting foreign to your experience? Don't let it be. Fasting is an aggressive way to affirm the promised

power of the spirit over the flesh. It is an explicit way
to reinforce the priority of prayer and to seek God
throughout each day. When facing crucial battles such
as the one that confronted Jehoshaphat, be ready to
deny the flesh as a sign that your trust is not in human
energy but in the power of the Spirit.

Next, the king and the people *prayed* (see 2 Chron.
20:6). And while their prayer confessed that "we have
no power" (20:12), it wasn't a "poor me" prayer! Instead of whining, their prayer roared, ascribing to
God power and authority over the enemy. Such a
prayer of petition is admittedly prayed out of deep
need, but it nonetheless boldly affirms God's power
within His will.

Third, there was also a *remembrance of God's work*
in history (see 2 Chron. 20:7). With praise they remembered the story of God's people—the Exodus
from Egypt, God's care in the wilderness, the con-
quest of Canaan. Remembering is a mighty source of
confidence that God is able and will again deliver
and save. Reviewing testimonies at the Lord's Table is
a great way for us to remember His tender mercies
and enduring love.

And fourth, there was a *prophetic utterance* (see
2 Chron. 20:14-17). We must be open to the Holy

Spirit's prophetic word among us as a people. He's still assuring us, "The battle is not yours, but God's!" (20:15) and He will faithfully unfold God's will for us in our own immediate situations.

Uncommonly threatening situations call for an uncommonly strong response: taking up a two-edged sword in a spiritual sense—*aggressively* trusting God, *forcefully* throwing ourselves at His feet in worship, and *boldly* brandishing the spiritual weapons Jehoshaphat used. They still work to put doubt and fear and anxiety to flight.

Praise is not passive. It can be our boldest stand against the threats of the enemy.

praise in prayer

O God my strength, I praise You for coming to me in my weakness. Grant that I may not use my humanity as a cloak for cowardice, but teach me to boldly affirm Your power to give me Your victory over the enemy. In Jesus' name, amen.

selected readings

Psalm 138   Acts 4:13-31

praise in practice

1. Has God ever come to your aid in the midst of some crisis you were facing? If so, recount what happened.

2. If you have ever fasted, describe your experience. Did it help you focus on the spirit over the flesh? What advice about fasting would you offer someone else who is considering it?

3. How can you discern when God wants you to relax and let Him work in your life and when He is calling for aggressive action on your part?

4. What do you think of the old saying that we should pray as though everything depended on God, and work as though everything depended on us?

The offerings of worship

*Give to the LORD, O families of the peoples,
give to the LORD glory and strength. Give to the LORD
the glory due His name; bring an offering, and
come into His courts.*

PSALM 96:7-8

It is impossible to talk about worship in a biblical framework without talking about offering to God our material substance—our money. This isn't because He needs our wealth, any more than He needs us to feed His ego with our praise. But the fact is, giving our financial resources is a proper response that opens the way to our functioning in the fundamental spiritual law of giving and receiving. *Giving* generously is the measure of how generously we can *receive*—how open we are to the inpouring of God's blessing.

The apostle Paul taught this to the Corinthians when he reminded them of the financial gifts he was soliciting for the impoverished, famine-ridden saints in Judea: "But this I say: He who sows sparingly will also reap sparingly, and he who sows bountifully will also reap bountifully" (2 Cor. 9:6). You see, God wants to pour His blessings into our lives, but our capacity to receive them depends on whether we "let out the plug" at the giving end of our lives. God created us to be channels of blessing, but our ability to receive the resources with which He wants us to bless others depends on our being able to give them away—freely, faithfully, generously. Here's the process: (1) He provides, (2) we trust and give, (3) He blesses our gifts to others, and then (4) He fills us again with His abundant provision.

King David understood this principle well. After God commanded David to make a special sacrifice, the angel of the Lord directed him to erect an altar on the nearby threshing floor of Ornan the Jebusite (see 1 Chron. 21:18). When David asked Ornan how much the site was worth, Ornan protested that he wanted to give it to the king for nothing—along with the oxen for the burnt offering and the threshing implements for the firewood (21:23). But knowing the law of giving and receiving, David replied, "No, but I will surely buy it for the full price, for I will not take what is yours for the LORD, nor offer burnt offerings with that which costs me nothing" (21:24).

At times, the Israelites proved the validity of this law in a negative way. During a time when they were feeling the absence of God, the prophet Malachi explained the problem to them: their neglect of giving was blocking their way. They had been robbing God of tithes and offerings. God prescribed the remedy: "Bring all the tithes into the storehouse, . . . [and see] if I will not open for you the windows of heaven and pour out for you such blessing that there will not be room enough to receive it" (Mal. 3:10).

Again, God summons our tithes as a part of praise-filled worship, not because He is out of money, nor even essentially because Christian work requires our funds. Our tithes are *first* a token of how much we truly honor Him with praise-filled hearts and lives. Offerings given to God are a gauge of whether we can be commended like the churches of Macedonia, who "first gave *themselves* to the Lord" (2 Cor. 8:5, emphasis added).

God's intended blessings of material resources are far more abundant than we can imagine or can ever repay. Let praiseful, obedient giving break any freeloading spirit, and according to His generosity and grace, let us worship with abounding financial gifts of our gratitude.

praise in prayer

God of good and gracious gifts, I praise You for blessing me with so many good things. Increase my capacity to be content with what I receive, and as You help me become a generous giver, make me an example of one that You can trust to give abundantly as You increase my ability to praise You in this way. Through Him who gave His all for me, amen.

selected readings

Matthew 6:25-34   2 Corinthians 9:6-15

praise in practice

1. Many Christians can bear witness to the way God responds to sacrifice with an outpouring of blessings. Can you think of such a time in your life when your sacrificial giving encouraged others to believe God's promise to bless those who "seek first the kingdom" (Matt. 6:33)?
2. Determine to pause during each day for a week to consciously focus on God's good gifts. Breathe in deeply as you praise God for His blessings; breathe out fully as you determine to share His gifts with others.
3. With the help of a concordance or Bible dictionary, make a study of tithing. Is it just an Old Testament ordinance, or does it apply to Christians?

The Lord's Beauty salon

Praise the LORD! For it is good to sing praises to our God;
for it is pleasant, and praise is beautiful.

PSALM 147:1

I have often said that if you want to become a handsome or a beautiful person, praise the Lord! You may know people who have lived in the presence of the Lord so long and who love Him so much that they begin to prove the truth of this psalm: "praise is beautiful." Their very demeanor speaks of the beauty of holiness, and their countenance evidences the beautifying power of praise.

Do you remember our words in the introduction to these studies—comments about our becoming more and more like the One we worship? This clearly is an important principle to our Father, because twice He says, both in Psalm 115:8 and 135:18, that those who worship idols "are like them." But the same is true of those of us who steadfastly look into the face of the Lord until His countenance begins to be mirrored in ours: His grace fashions us into gracious people, and His beauty transforms our own countenances.

Now, "beautiful" may not be your first thought when you get up in the morning and stare into the mirror. Stress, tragedy or deep sorrow may have etched creases of weariness or suffering on your face. But try this experiment—prove God's Word. Take that countenance, as it is, into the presence of the

Lord day after day in frequent, steadfast praise and worship. The prophet Isaiah says plainly what you will receive in return. He promises that the Servant of the Lord, the One who turned out to be the Messiah, is sent specifically "to console those who mourn in Zion, to give them beauty for ashes, the oil of joy for mourning" (Isa. 61:3). That's an oil with amazing results that surpasses any temporal rejuvenating effect of human cosmetics!

In biblical times, ashes were a sign of grief and mourning. When Abraham dared to intercede on behalf of the wicked city of Sodom, he said to God, "I who am but dust and ashes have taken it upon myself to speak to the Lord" (Gen. 18:27). When Tamar was defiled by her half-brother Amnon, she put ashes on her head and tore her robe in anguish (see 2 Sam. 13:19). Job sat in ashes as a sign of his desperate plight (see Job 2:8), and later when God confronted him, Job said, "I abhor myself, and repent in dust and ashes" (42:6). Ashes could signify deep humility or even insignificance.

Now comes the promised Servant predicted by Isaiah—Jesus the Lord! He sees people in ashes—people uncertain about God, devoid of hope, oppressed by the realization of their own imperfection and weakness. What a desolate picture! How unlovely we *all* are without the Messiah! But—whisper that word expectantly—*but* His love and mercy offer the perfect sin offering on the altar of God. From the ashes of His offering, a marvelous transformation affects the souls *and the faces* of those who accept that love and mercy. The inner beauty of Christ Himself begins to shine. Forgiven, their pinched and anguished faces relax in God's peace. Loved, their countenances glow. Caught up in praise, they worship "in the beauty of holiness" (Ps. 29:2) Through the world's most marvelous miracle, they—indeed, *we!*—have been given beauty in the place of ashes.

praise in prayer

Beautiful Savior, I love to gaze upon You and to feel Your love becoming a part of who I am. I honor You above all beautiful things in heaven and on Earth, just for who You are, and for Your power to touch even sordid lives and transform them into beautiful people. We praise You in Jesus' name, amen.

selected readings

Psalm 48   Isaiah 61

praise in practice

1. Describe someone you know, perhaps an older person, who seems to have an inner beauty that comes from knowing and worshiping the Lord.
2. Many parents have said to their daughters the old saying "Pretty is as pretty does." How does this also express a Christian truth?
3. Do you think there is too much emphasis on external beauty in our society? In the Church?
4. What traits do you think best characterize a spiritually beautiful person?

singing with the spirit and the understanding

Sing praises to God, sing praises! Sing praises to our King, sing praises! For God is the King of all the earth; sing praises with understanding.

PSALM 47:6-7

There is no shortage of songs in the world, but not all of them praise God. In fact, many parents are understandably concerned about the corrupting influence of some music—and especially the sensual or violent lyrics bombarding youth today.

Anna and I were very concerned about one such song that our son was required to sing at his grade school graduation exercises. It was a New Age rock piece and included words that were hardly edifying. After the ceremony, I asked our son about it—not criticizing him at all, because I trusted him. I was simply probing to see to what degree he had been paying attention to the pagan lyrics the class had sung together. "How did you feel about singing that song?" I asked.

"Oh, that," this 12-year-old said. "I don't even know all the words, Dad. I just heard enough when we started practicin' it—ya' could tell it wasn't the kinda' song that we'd sing. Anyway, after that I stopped singin' the words, an' when everyone else sang, I'd just sing in the Spirit!"

It was so terrific! He was just a boy, but he already knew the difference between "the song of the Lord" and the songs of the world, and he realized the benefit of appropriating the spiritual song. And best of all, the lyrics of that song did matter to him!

Music mattered to the psalmist too, who admonished Israel to sing "with understanding" (Ps. 47:7). Later, the apostle Paul would echo this teaching: "I will sing with the spirit, and I will also sing with the understanding" (1 Cor. 14:15). Paul was especially concerned that those in the congregation gifted with songs in a tongue granted by the Holy Spirit also render them in a language that visitors could understand.

Yet in our own assemblies today, how often, even in our own language, are songs merely mouthed—without vital understanding. In such instances, it hardly matters how holy or filled with the Spirit the songwriter was. The composer's Spirit-fullness is no substitute for each would-be worshiper's singing with understanding.

Further, we all need discernment in the presentation of Christian music. Perhaps you, as I, have been around the music of worship long enough to appreciate the need for Spirit-led and sensitively ministered worship in song. Periodically, some artists lose their bearings and become more preoccupied with verifying their status as being as good as secular musicians and forget their primary ministry to the Lord. I am certainly not saying that we shouldn't cultivate our best talents and hone our skills to the sharpest as we offer our music to God. I'm simply affirming the obvious: Holy Spirit enablement, joined to sensitivity in understanding, can cause a song to soar. A song born of such balance can better flow to God's honor and glory through a dedicated, single-minded heart than through a technically accurate but double-minded musician whose spirit is not in tune with *the* Spirit.

Someone once said to a leader at our church, "I don't know what Pastor Jack is doing, having us spend so much time singing. I guess *he* just likes it." The truth is, we do nothing in our gatherings just because I or anyone else "likes it." We've targeted larger purposes than private taste. The music the gathered Church raises to God is crucial to what happens *among* us as well as *in* us. Our singing is not a preliminary warm-up to the "main event" called the sermon. Rather, our songs are an integral part of the worship, made vibrantly alive *in* us as we sing with the Spirit and with the understanding also (see 1 Cor. 14:15). It speaks to obtaining godly wisdom to learn such a way.

praise in prayer

We praise You, Lord, for the song You have put in our hearts and for the musical gifts that enliven our assemblies. Grant that our minds and spirits will be in tune with Your eternal will. Through Jesus Christ our Lord, amen.

selected readings

Psalm 33:1-5   Acts 16:25-34

praise in practice

1. Take a look at a hymnbook and examine the words of some of the old standby favorites to see if you understand all the lyrics. Look especially at "Night with Ebon Pinion" (what kind of night is that?) and "Come Thou Fount of Every Blessing" (what is an "Ebenezer"?).

2. Read Ephesians 5:17-21 and Colossians 3:16. According to these passages, what

are the characteristics, purpose and result of singing, and what kinds of songs are to be used in worship?

3. Enjoy a time of singing favorite "spiritual songs."

praise: The weapon of our warfare

Your hand will find all Your enemies; Your right hand will find those who hate You. Be exalted, O LORD, in Your own strength! We will sing and praise Your power.

PSALM 21:8,13

some people have trouble with passages in the psalms that pray for God to deal violently with the enemies of His people. While there is a difference between some Old Testament attitudes and the teaching of Christ to love our enemies, the Psalms are not totally vengeful and vindictive. In general, the Old Testament makes a distinction between taking revenge ourselves and leaving our enemies to God. Strength and power lie in Him, not in us, as Psalm 21 confesses.

The role of praise in dealing with our enemies is also strange to many people. There are many good reasons for glorifying and worshiping God—His sheer magnitude and magnificence, the fact that He is our Redeemer and that He commanded us to praise Him—and that praise is healthy and healing to the whole person. But the psalmist also praises God in the midst of facing adversity at the hand of an enemy. Do you wonder how such conflict and praise meet?

The relationship is explained from a human standpoint in what is one of the strangest stories in the history of warfare. This story brings us back to 2 Chronicles 20 and King Jehoshaphat. Remember, Jehoshaphat and the kingdom of Judah are teetering on the brink of destruction—they are about to be attacked by a horde far outnumbering them. You might compare their plight to a situation of your own in which everything seems to go wrong, or when the force of Satan's opposition threaten to overpower you. King Jehoshaphat's experience offers a way to do battle in such situations. He begins by simply confessing, "We have no power against this great multitude that is coming against us" (2 Chron. 20:12).

This confession of weakness doesn't mean that Judah is passive and does nothing—nor should we. A prophet of Judah delivers a word from the Lord. God tells them that the battle is His, not theirs. For their response, the people "[stand] up to praise the LORD God of Israel with voices loud and high" (2 Chron. 20:19). Then, instead of hurling spears or boulders, the army marches out, boldly hurling phrases of praises, singing, "Praise the LORD, for His mercy endures forever" (20:21). The result? The Lord Himself sets ambushes for the enemy, causing confusion and fighting to break out among their ranks. The result? An utter rout!

So what attack should believers mount against Satan and his hordes? We are to take up the weapons we wield best—the weapons of praise. As the apostle Paul teaches us, "the weapons of our warfare are not carnal but mighty in God for pulling down strongholds" (2 Cor. 10:4).

Faced with the forces of evil, God's people are not to fear. Our greatest resource for resistance doesn't arise from any arsenal known to human wisdom or device. It comes from knowing that the battle is the Lord's. We are never to react from a position of weakness, but from one of strength. That strength is found in faithfully remaining at our post of praise. Our best defense is to do what we should know how to do best: offer praise and glory to the Living God, whose enemies, ultimately, will always flee before His might and power.

praise in prayer

You know my human weaknesses, O God.
You know that I live in a world in which the
strength of praise is scoffed at and considered to
be weakness. Catch me up in the realm of
spiritual truth so that in difficult situations
I may remain at my post of praise. Through
Jesus Christ, my victorious Lord, amen.

selected Readings

Psalm 147:1-11   Revelation 19:1-7

praise in practice

1. What is your first reaction likely to be when someone attacks you, either verbally or physically? Does praising the Lord as a line of defense seem to be totally unrealistic?

2. On a 3x5 card, write encouraging words such as, "The weapon of His people is praise." Carry the card with you in your pocket or purse for a couple of days, taking it out and reading it frequently to refresh your memory. Then discuss with a friend whether this exercise has helped to impress the truth of today's reflection on your mind.

The Kind of Worship God Blesses

Behold, how good and how pleasant it is for brethren to dwell together in unity! It is like the dew of Hermon, descending upon the mountains of Zion; for there the LORD commanded the blessing—life forevermore.

PSALM 133:1,3

"That service really blessed me!"

It's good to hear such responses after a gathering for public worship. Often such remarks are the result of the free flow of the Spirit, symbolized in the Scriptures as an anointing like the one that is referred to in this psalm (see Ps. 133:2). Moving music ministry, testimonies, and healthy Bible teaching are also anointed; but in Psalm 133, it is *corporate unity* that receives the anointing and God's appointed blessing. Have we given sufficient attention to the unity of the Body as a key proviso—as an avenue through which God has chosen to bless His people?

We may have to use our imagination some to appreciate the imagery of this psalm. To say that unity is as pleasant as oil running down Aaron's head on to his beard and garments (see Ps. 133:2) may sound a little strange to us. But if you've ever been involved in a congregation torn apart by division, you can easily make the connection between the blessing of Church harmony and the refreshment of early morning dew atop a mountain in a hot Mediterranean climate (see 133:3).

As churches today move into worship renewal, it's not uncommon for them to experience some struggle and strain. Old traditions may be disrupted. Understanding about what worship leaders are attempting may be slow in coming. Although each fellowship must work through these issues in its own way, I've found that there are five elements usually present when the Body successfully negotiates the waters of renewal.

There is first of all a general *willingness* for the worship to be rescued from spirit-deadening routine to Spirit-led vitality. Unfortunately, like taking medicine, it's sometimes necessary for us to hurt before we want to change. People who see nothing wrong with worship as it always has been may not hurt enough to be willing to change.

For unified worship renewal to take place, *sensitivity* must characterize a substantial number of congregants and worship. They must have an instinct for what God wants and for what best enables people to render publicly what they feel for God in their hearts.

There must be widespread *understanding* if the Body is to move forward together in worship. Here the responsibility of teachers and preachers cannot be overemphasized. God's people will generally respond positively to changes that are shown to be grounded in the Word and will of God.

The leaders must have a certain *alertness* to congregational reaction, especially if they are attempting innovation in worship. This doesn't mean that pastors are to be ruled by the whim of the majority. It does mean that they are ministers to the *Body*, not just ministers of God. If they are disinterested in the whole process of worship renewal or if they are blind to whether what happens in worship is really accomplishing renewal, unified worship is impossible.

And let's face it: for the Body to respond in unity, there must be a certain level of *ability* on the part of worship leaders. This is not an appeal for slick and skillful techniques. It is an appeal for offering our best in worship. God was not pleased when His Old Covenant people offered sacrifices of blemished animals. And neither He nor His New Covenant people respond favorably to sloppy and careless worship leadership today.

Are you doing your part to make the corporate worship of the Body so pleasantly unified that it's a true *anointing*?

praise in prayer

*We praise You, Father, Son and Holy Spirit,
for the unity You manifest. We repent of the
disunity manifested among Your people, and
we pray for a renewed willingness to accept
the unity of the Spirit in the bond of peace.
Through Christ we pray, amen.*

selected readings

Romans 15:1-7   Ephesians 4:1-16

praise in practice

1. In Romans 15:5-6, what specific *result* of a
   spirit of unity is anticipated?
2. Suppose you are a part of a church whose
   members have a wide variety of personal
   preferences when it comes to worship
   styles. Make a list of the factors that
   would be required to keep the Body unified during a time of worship renewal.

The Christ of the psalms: King of kings

*I will declare the decree: the LORD has said to Me,
"You are My Son, today I have begotten You. Ask of Me,
and I will give You the nations for Your inheritance, and
the ends of the earth for Your possession."*

PSALM 2:7-8; 24:9-10

one of the unique features of the psalms is David's praise of one greater—one to come. Over and over devout Jews would ask of this passage— and others like it—"of whom does the prophet speak?" While David was God's son in the created sense, as we are, the Holy Spirit gave David words about another Son in an "only begotten" sense, a sense beyond what he may have understood. The world would have to wait until Jesus the Messiah came to hear it explained that "my Lord" and "my Son" actually and ultimately refer to Jesus Christ Himself (see Heb. 1:5,10).

This unique feature of the Psalms makes them an appropriate vehicle for us to praise the uniqueness of Christ. So pause with me. Let's just spend time focusing on how there is none other like Jesus. The following is excerpted from a sermon on His uniqueness, which I brought to nearly 3,000 leaders in England.

Jesus is the one and only Second Adam, sent to salvage and restore what the First Adam lost.

He is the unique virgin-born Son of God, sinless Man; He is the Incarnate Truth, the manifest fullness of the Father.

He is the only substitutionary Lamb of God—dying according to the Scriptures and given to redeem from sin all who believe in His name.

Jesus is the Crucified One who was buried and who rose again—literally, physically and in power—on the third day, according to the Scriptures.

He is the One and only One who, upon completely providing the grounds of all human redemption, has ascended to heaven to take His seat at the right hand of the Father.

He is the One who has poured out the Holy Spirit upon all those who obey Him.

He is the One who ever lives to make intercession for us.

He is the One who will soon descend and be revealed as King of kings and Lord of lords, to receive His redeemed Church to be with Him forever.

His alone is the blood that can redeem; His alone the body broken for our healing; His alone is the sacrifice that can satisfy the price of atonement for sin; His alone the death that can purchase life for sinful man. His alone is the righteousness that can justify us before God, establishing us as not guilty in

His court; His alone the power that can break the chains of death—for it was not possible that He could be held by death; and He alone, in rising, has verified to us the promise of eternal life.

Soldiers sent to capture Him returned saying, "We've never heard any man speak like this man."

Disciples witnessing Him stilling the storm said, "Who can this be, that even the wind and the sea obey Him!"

The Roman centurion, having watched Him die, declared, "Truly this was the Son of God!"

Thomas, at first doubting, was led finally to confess that in the resurrected Jesus he saw "my Lord and my God!"

God? Yes, for this is the One and only One who is enthroned far above all principalities and power and might and dominion, and every name that is named, not only in this age but also in the world to come.

Throughout the Psalms there is an interplay between David, king of Israel, and, in a prophetic sense, Christ—*the* King from whom David received his own throne. In Psalm 24, the rich imagery is of a great king approaching a city under his control. As he and his colorful entourage approach the city gates, their presence is so commanding that the gates—the city leaders who gathered there in counsel—are exhorted to attend to their entry. The city and its inhabitants are to make the royal party welcome. In writing, David proposes a royal welcome for the King of heaven.

Are the gates to our hearts prepared to give such honor to the entry and enthronement of Christ, our King of Glory? The question needs to be asked not because kingship is so unusual in our own days, but because it is so common! That is, the number of those who assume *sovereignty*—the claim to rule—is almost equal to the number of free-willed human beings who walk the earth. Yet, though sovereignty abounds, the King of Glory will tolerate no competition.

Not only do states, nations, kingdoms and governments claim sovereignty over individuals, individuals themselves also claim sovereignty over their own lives. No cry has been louder in our day than the demand for self-determination. And indeed, such freedom is a God-endowed privilege invested in all persons by virtue of their having been created in the image of God.

But the *misapplication* of sovereignty is widespread, too, and this makes it all the more important that we identify the uniqueness of Christ's sovereignty. "Taking control of my own life," a mantra we often hear, must be affirmed only under the superior rule of the King of Glory.

Christ is King by virtue of His being *the source of creation*. John's Gospel begins by recalling Genesis 1: God speaks the universe into existence and names Jesus as the creative Word behind it all (see John 1:1-3,14). And in the Revelation, royal worshipers cast their own crowns aside, saying, "You are worthy, O Lord, to receive glory and honor and power; for You created all things" (Rev. 4:11).

Christ is King because He is *God's only begotten Son*. His royal status was recognized by other royalty at His birth, as the wise men from the East inquired, "Where is He who has been born King of the Jews?" (Matt. 2:2). And toward the end of His earthly life, His kingship was pictured in the triumphal entry into the city of Jerusalem, in fulfillment of the prophecy, "Behold, your King is coming to you, lowly, and sitting on a donkey, a colt, the foal of a donkey" (Matt. 21:5).

That Christ is King was *announced by Peter at Pentecost* as he proclaimed Jesus raised from the dead and exalted to the right hand of the throne of God! (see Acts 2:32-36).

And Christ the King will come again from that throne in royal power. Thus it is *before Him* that all humankind will finally appear for review and judgment. Thus it is *by Him* that every person will be measured and either approved or disapproved. And thus it is *unto Him* that every being shall ultimately bow the knee and that every tongue shall confess that Jesus Christ is Lord, to the glory of the Father.

Let every ear hear it! Let every heart-gate open freely for His entry, confessing with mind and heart and body, "You are the Christ, the Son of the living God. You alone are King of kings, and Lord of hosts!"

praise in prayer

I exalt You, Lord Jesus, as the unique Son, as King of kings and Lord of lords. I confess that there is no other name in heaven or on Earth by which we can be saved. I praise You, King of heaven, for exercising Your power with such

*love and justice. I adore You, Lord over all
the earth, for the blessings You distribute so
freely to Your subjects. I honor You, King Jesus,
as master of my life. Help my life to reflect my
acknowledgment of You as my personal King.
In Your own name, amen.*

selected readings

Psalm 47   Hebrews 1

praise in practice

1. What implications does Christ's uniqueness have as far as our priorities and loy-
   alties are concerned? For evangelism?
2. What implication for the self-image of the
   Christian can be drawn from the fact that
   Christ is king (see Rev. 1:5-6)?
3. What part of our lives do we (do *you!*) have
   most difficulty subjecting to the kingship
   of Jesus?

You can't escape Him—and aren't you glad!

*Where can I go from Your Spirit? Or where can
I flee from Your presence? If I ascend into heaven,
You are there; if I make my bed in hell,
behold, You are there.*

PSALM 139:7-8

This poignant psalm seems at first to convey the idea that the writer is in flight from God and His Spirit—like a spiritual fugitive trying to outrun the pursuit of a cosmic cop. Of course, the writer discovers that there is no escape. It would be foolish to expect to flee to heaven to hide from the Spirit, for that is His domain. Even hell cannot hide us from Him (the word "hell" in this verse is taken from *sheol*, which refers to the grave, not the place of everlasting punishment). The message is clear: God will find us, whether we are flying high or lying low.

Then, from an apparent context of despair, a strongly positive aspect appears. The psalmist's tone turns to the glad confession that God's omnipresent Spirit is not pursuing him to do him harm, but to lead and guide him (see Ps. 139:10). It's a wonderful advance note on the New Testament's unfolding of the comforting presence of the Holy Spirit: the Paraclete promised to "abide with you forever" (John 14:16). Our praise deserves to be regularly punctuated with continual gratitude for His real presence and power.

Against the spirit of a materialistic spiritually blinded age, in which so many neither perceive nor believe in anything that isn't physically perceptible or tangible, praise God with me for the Holy Spirit!

The psalmist's refreshing reminder that the Spirit is *omnipresent* (i.e., *everywhere!*) is a precious truth. It announces to us: You will be besieged by *no* state of mind, pursued by *no* terror and threatened by *no* imprisoning effect of hell that the Spirit cannot penetrate, conquer or overthrow!

Our human nature may at times feel embarrassed at this inescapable presence, wishing we could hide our darker actions and thoughts. But in our wisest moments, or most desperate, we rejoice in the fact that He pursues us, especially in times when weakness or temptation ambushes us.

Let every believer praise God for the Holy Spirit's being *our Helper in prayer*. "For we do not know what we should pray for as we ought, but the Spirit Himself makes intercession for us with groanings which cannot be uttered . . . according to the will of God" (Rom. 8:26-27).

Let every believer praise God for the overwhelming *power* of the Spirit. He is *the* Force—the *real* one—not the cultish or ethereal "Force" of a *Star Wars* flick. He is the personally caring, mightily attentive-to-us Holy Spirit of God! He "was hovering over the face of the waters" when the creation was spoken into existence (Gen. 1:2), He was the One who came upon

Jesus at His baptism (see Matt. 3:16), and He's the
One who still baptizes believers today with empow-
ering grace (see Luke 24:49 and Acts 2:4).

Let every believer praise God for the Spirit's
indwelling and leading in our everyday lives, for the
freedom His presence brings from oppressive religious rules, and for the rich fruit He begets—the love
and joy, the peace and patience He produces in the
life of the committed Christian (see Gal. 5:16-26).

In all these and a host of other ways, the Holy
Spirit is our assurance; He makes real a higher and
deeper realm than the mere material world about us.
Yet He is so practical, and life in the Spirit is so work-
able in a workaday world. He has not called us to some
disembodied existence in order to make us spiritual;
rather, His power permeates our daily reality with the
new wine of renewal, and He is fully available to each
of us who *asks* for His presence (see Luke 11:13).

Who would *ever* want to flee from *that* presence?!

praise in prayer

Holy Spirit, I praise You for surrounding me with Your abiding presence and dynamic availability. Help me to live in the power of Your indwelling and fullness, and to walk in simple, trusting dependence on Your promised guidance. In Jesus' name, amen.

selected Readings

Psalm 139:1-18   John 16:5-15

praise in practice

1. Why is it important to refer to the Holy Spirit as "He" (as in John 16:5-15), instead of "it"?
2. What evidence have you experienced of the reality of the Holy Spirit?
3. Do you think even Christians are sometimes tempted to think of reality in terms of the merely material?

wanted: Hearts where the comforter can Abide

Reproach has broken my heart, and I am full of heaviness; I looked for someone to take pity, but there was none; and for comforters, but I found none.

PSALM 69:20

once more, David's plight becomes an avenue of praise. In his flight from the jealous rages of Saul, David had sought comfort and refuge with Ahimelech, priest of Nob (see 1 Sam. 21:1-9); with Achish, king of Gath (see 21:10-15); even with Israel's arch enemies, the Philistines (see 27:1-7). Yet he had found no comforter like the Lord, and he can finally say, "Let heaven and earth praise Him. . . . For God will save Zion" (Ps. 69:34-35).

Under the New Covenant, the role of Comforter (Paraclete) belongs to the Holy Spirit. Five times in John's Gospel, Jesus promised specific benefits from this Paraclete—which literally means one who has been "called alongside" to act both as a comforter and an advocate. First, knowing that He would shortly be returning to the Father, Jesus promised that the Spirit Comforter, or Helper, would *abide* with us forever (see John 14:16). Praise God for the continuing presence of the indwelling, overflowing work of the Holy Spirit, given to us as a pledge of the glory to come when Jesus returns (see 2 Cor. 1:22).

Second, Jesus promised that the Comforter would *teach* His disciples, bringing to their remembrance His words and guiding them into all truth (see John 14:26; 16:13). We can hardly imagine how bereft the disciples of Jesus would have been, and how impoverished we would be, had not the divine Helper inspired them to recall and record the teaching of Jesus in what has become the the New Testament. Further, though of less authority than the absolute finality of the written Word, the Church still continues to receive truth through the Spirit's gift of prophecy. These words are greatly enabling, helping us to respond to new situations in the power and wisdom of the Spirit's prompting and edification (see Rom. 12:6; 1 Cor. 12:10; Eph. 4:11).

Third, the Comforter would also *testify* of Jesus (see John 15:26). He does this by animating our witness and by confirming the Word of the gospel with signs of power and grace. The Holy Spirit has unlimited power to demonstrate through the Church that *Jesus is still alive* and well and that His Kingdom power is unrestricted by either the flesh or the devil.

Fourth, Jesus promised that the Helper would "*convict* the world of sin, and of righteousness, and of judgment" (John 16:9-11, emphasis added). The Holy Spirit works to convince and convict hearts that Jesus is Lord and Savior—a task impossible for mere humans, because only He sees into human hearts and can give them a full awareness of their need.

And finally, John records Jesus' promise that the Comforter would *glorify* Him. After Jesus' departure to the Father, the Holy Spirit forged His divine qualities into protective armor and sanctified character, and then He clothed Jesus' followers with them to equip them to continue His ministry (see John 16:14-15).

What thrilling promises! Yet there is a condition. The construction of the original language in these five promises from John's Gospel indicates that *each of the last four ministries of the Comforter depends on our receptivity to the first.* That is, we will never benefit from the Holy Spirit's work in our lives unless we are completely open to His *abiding,* or *dwelling,* in us.

There is a sobering and practical point to all this: the growth of both the Church and our own lives—as well as the impact of spiritual renewal on our souls, however grand it may have been—has no guaranteed future on its own momentum. Resting on past successes will not qualify us to claim the future for God. Only by praying for fresh anointings of the Spirit to sensitize us to fresh opportunities and responsibilities can we realize the benefits of the Comforter in the days ahead.

praise in prayer

We praise You, Holy Father, for the gift and the gifts of Your Holy Spirit. Oh, Spirit of God, grant that I may be receptive to Your steadfast abiding work in me, so that I may be a part of Your continuing ministry in my day, my home, my church family and my world. In Your name, amen.

selected readings

1 Corinthians 12:1-11   Galatians 5:16-26

praise in practice

1. Take several moments to respond to Luke 11:13 in prayer, simply asking the Lord for a fuller measure of His Holy Spirit.
2. What life changes characterize those who are filled with the Spirit (see Gal. 5:16-26)?

The power of weakness before the awesome God

O God, You are more awesome than
Your holy places. The God of Israel is He who gives
strength and power to His people.

PSALM 68:35

I'm sure that if we knew more of the truth
about the awesome God, we would react
something like Isaiah, whom we studied earli-
er. Return again to Isaiah 6, to the great scene that
demonstrates the transforming power of standing
before Him whom the psalmist calls "awesome" (Ps.
68:35). There is no more awe-inspiring scene in the
Bible than this Throne Room confrontation with the
thrice holy God.

Daunted by the pure holiness of God's dazzling
robes, the strange creatures around His throne, the
shaking doorposts, and the echo of the cry "Holy,
holy, holy" (Isa. 6:3), Isaiah seems melted. He is able
only to say, "Woe is me" (6:5).

I doubt that the fullest worship of our hearts can
occur without our understanding something of the
overwhelming anxiety that we can imagine in Isaiah's
voice. How else could anyone feel, standing in
human imperfection before ultimate Perfectness?
But in what has to be one of the most profound para-
doxes in human experience, Isaiah emerges from the
heavenly Throne Room as a man of vision, direction,
strength and mission.

We might say that Isaiah, a sinful man, was able to
stand his ground in life only after being swept off his

feet by God. And something like that should happen to us—to you, to me!—in worship. The trembling gives way to trust. We discover that His supreme power is to some extent transferable. It soon becomes apparent that our insufficiency is swallowed up in His all-sufficiency.

You see, God did not summon Isaiah to His throne to scare the stamina out of Him. God plays no games as a smoke-machine-pumping Wizard of Oz. Rather, God calls us to worship, and there He wants to display His might, because He knows we will face tasks in which we need to act mightily. He wants to supplant our unholiness with His holiness, our unwholeness with His wholeness. He is not disposed to *frighten us to death* for entering His presence, but to *awe us to life* because we have been in His presence. The Ground of All Being wants us to be able to stand our ground in life's trials. To do so in the face of sorrow, temptation, illness and disappointments requires that we frequently visit the holy place. The God who is so much more awesome Himself than the appointments that awed Isaiah waits there to fill us with a part of Himself.

We must never hesitate to come to the awesome God, though we come in our weakness. Let us borrow from His divine strength and then honor and praise the Source of our healing. Let us be taught by the parable of the prodigal son in Luke 15. Not only is the forgiving love of the Father taught there, but the son, having flouted his regard for his father at first, later remembers and acknowledges the source of his security. His return to "home" is wonderful, but more awesome than the place is the person—his father. And he has come to him, just as we have been invited to come before the Father.

Never believe that you are still too down and weak to come to Him. Remember, He's waiting—God is waiting in the Throne Room—not to resist or dispel you, but to receive and reward you with strength sufficient for every tomorrow. Bring Him your fears and find new fearlessness in fearing Him. Bring Him your weakness and find strength in His might.

praise in prayer

Holy Father, I would not dare to come into Your presence without Your having called me to come, and without the covering of the blood of Jesus. I honor You and magnify Your name, asking only that I may be strengthened by being in Your presence. Through Christ my Lord, amen.

selected Readings

Isaiah 66:1-2   Hebrews 12:18-29

praise in practice

1. Was your earliest remembered awareness of God frightening or reassuring?

2. As a parent or Sunday School teacher, plan how you can help children under your influence grasp something of both the awesomeness of God and of His willingness to strengthen us.

3. Do the assemblies where you worship foster a sense of the awesomeness and holiness of God? How is this best done?

DAY 24

understanding the Heart of God

*He heals the brokenhearted and binds up
their wounds. He counts the number of the stars;
He calls them all by name. Great is our Lord, and
mighty in power; His understanding is infinite.
The LORD lifts up the humble.*

PSALM 147:3-6

How grand to praise a God whose vast understanding encompasses the names of the stars *and* whose detailed attentiveness in love knows each individual heart and need as well! How magnificently this text asserts the grandeur of God's love—how it reveals His heart *to lift up* the sinful and not to *put them down.*

This knowledge was made clearest to us all when Jesus came and transformed and rearranged humankind's view of God. Jesus repeatedly told parables that countered our confused picture of the Father. In three of these parables, Jesus dealt with the human inclination to focus more on our guilt than on God's grace: the stories of the lost *sheep,* the lost *coin* and the lost *son*—all recorded in Luke 15.

The parable of the lost sheep (see Luke 15:1-7) reveals that in the heart of God *no one is unimportant.* God is never so preoccupied with "safe" (saved) people that He is unconcerned about the one person at risk. God *counts* His sheep. If He has a flock of 100 and notices that only 99 trot into the fold at night, He doesn't say, "Too bad—one scoundrel is missing!" Rather, He goes out at night into the wilderness to find that one solitary lamb; when He finally finds it, He puts it on His shoulders and returns home rejoicing.

Whatever guilt or aloneness you may feel, take time to look, listen and praise God that you are a precious sheep in His eyes!

The parable of the lost coin (see Luke 15:8-10) shows God's glad anticipation of being reunited in a working partnership with us. In the parable, the reason for the woman's eagerness to find the lost silver coin is that it was on the order of an engagement ring—part of a set of 10 coins woven together and worn as a necklace at her wedding.

What is the significance of this story for us? Often, shamed by our sin, we may run or hide from God, not only oblivious to His *love* but also unaware that He sees us as desirable—as needed to complete a set. He has plans for a partnership with us, plans that will be crippled without us. Whatever our shame or sense of unworthiness, let us remember how much we are desired and valued by the Father's heart.

Last, the familiar parable of the lost son (see Luke 15:11-24) shows God's plans for the *complete restoration* of the lost. This glimpse into God's heart reveals a Father who is *waiting* for the son's return. The father does not require the prodigal boy to grovel at his feet, gives no half-hearted acceptance of the son's approach, and does not hold his son at arm's length to test his sincerity. Instead, there is a warm, glad and immediate embrace, the presentation of the best robe, the gift of a gold ring and sandals, and a jubilant "welcome home" party. However distant you may feel or have been, believe this: The Father will welcome you home—gladly!

As we consider these stories in light of the passage that opened this devotional, we can easily imagine that David was the author of Psalm 147. There are the references to Jerusalem, the city David loved, and to the harp, which David played. Most significant, however, is the fact that David himself had been a wandering sheep who discovered that God would not abandon him; a lost coin that God longed to recover, and a prodigal son whom the Father joyously welcomed home to full restoration in the family.

Many of us can bear personal testimony to having discovered these traits of the infinitely gracious heart of God. Not only is it such a wonderful revelation that we praise Him for His love, but it is also amazing to discover that the more we praise Him, the more in-depth our understanding of His heart becomes. As a result, we are better equipped to relate these truths to others by our words, our love and our acceptance of them.

praise in prayer

Praise to You, dear Father, for valuing me in spite of my sin. Help me to rely on and respond fully to the richness of Your love so that I never hide from You but accept the wealth of Your wholehearted acceptance of me. Through Jesus I pray, amen.

selected readings

Luke 15:1-10   Luke 15:11-32

praise in practice

1. In your experience, does God's family, the Church, typically respond to returning prodigals more as the father did or as the elder brother did?
2. How do shame and embarrassment keep the guilty from returning to God?

Beyond Transcendence: Caught *up* to plunge *in*

The LORD is high above all nations, His glory above the heavens. Who is like the LORD our God, who dwells on high, who humbles Himself to behold the things that are in the heavens and in the earth?

PSALM 113:4-6

worship and praise by definition enable the worshiper to transcend the earthly plane. The psalmist's focus on a God who is "high above" lifts him out of discouragement and defeat, gives him a view from the mountaintop and allows him to see Earth from the perspective of heaven. This is not to say that the worshiper has been beamed up out of the world into an unreality or brought to the presence of a God who cannot be bothered with mundane human existence. But the God high above *is* a God who "raises the poor out of the dust, and lifts the needy out of the ash heap" (Ps. 113:7). He lifts us up through a worship that transcends the limits of our world in at least three ways.

Worship *transcends the temporal*. We want to learn to offer worship in season and out of season—with constancy and faithfulness instead of whimsy and fleeting feelings. It's amazing how becoming caught up in worship can make us say, "Where did the time go?!" True worship not only transcends time, it also lifts us beyond the limits of those things that time and life have engrained in our systems of thought and habit. Worship works to release us from the constraints that years of sin and bondage have woven and warped in us.

Worship *transcends the traditional*. Living worship is never static; rather, it always finds fresh, vital ways of expressing praise to God Most High. Without such transcendence, the finest worship patterns easily degenerate into rote recitations and deadening dullness. Of course, none of us lives without tradition, which can be an *en*abler of worship rather than a *dis*abler. Yet praying for the new wine of the Spirit requires us to be ready to find the old *re*newed—to stretch new wineskins that can contain God's renewing freshness.

True worship *transcends the theoretical*. Worship is not merely a cerebral, mystical or emotional experience. It is the humbling of the entire human being—body and mind, spirit and emotions—before the Creator-Redeemer. True worship transcends the vain supposition that human energy can get things going, recognizing that God is the source and foundation for all our becoming, doing and accomplishing.

Again, this emphasis on worship that transcends must not trick us into thinking that entering the Throne Room on high separates us *from* reality. In fact, it is an entrance *into* it. Worship catches us *up* to God, only to plunge us *into* and prepare us to deal *with* issues related to everyday life.

Remember, transcendent worship accompanied the commissioning of the early disciples to teach all nations (see Matt. 28:16-20). Transcendent worship accompanied the establishment of the Church (see Acts 2:1-14). Transcendent worship equipped the Christian martyr Stephen to endure stoning, with the prayer, "Lord, do not charge them with this sin" (Acts 7:60).

Let us never speak of the need to make worship relevant to life. Worship *is* life. Entering the Throne Room of God "high above" (Ps. 113:4) is an activity perfectly suited to earthbound people; it ennobles and enables us to deal with earthly situations in His transcendent power.

praise in prayer

Dear Father, blot forever from my mind
any notion or thinking that You dwell in a
far-off, other-worldly realm and that worshiping
You is not intimately related to my life in this
world. Grant that my visits to Your Presence will
only equip me to heal the hurts around me.
In Jesus' name, amen.

selected readings

Psalm 61   Isaiah 57:15-21

praise in practice

1. Reflect on the difference between *actually worshiping* and *thinking about* and *discussing* worship.
2. When faced with a problem or crisis, what is likely to be your first reaction? To act? To think about the problem and a possible solution? To pray? When might it be appropriate to act first?

keys to sustaining faith in difficult times

Save me, O God! For the waters have come up to my neck. I sink in deep mire, where there is no standing; . . . I am weary with my crying; my throat is dry; my eyes fail while I wait for my God.

PSALM 69:1-3

There is no weariness like the soul-weariness of which the psalmist speaks here. Quick surges of faith may occur in an inspirational moment, but how do you *sustain* faith during prolonged sickness, continued temptation or seemingly unending relational struggles? Here are six keys.

Feed on Living Bread. Jesus said, "Man shall not live by bread alone, but by every word that proceeds from the mouth of God" (Matt. 4:4). When you come to the end of yet another day that has drained your physical, emotional and spiritual strength, sit down and read the Word of God. If you can't stay awake, stand up and read it aloud. "But, Jack," you might be protesting, "that's the very time I don't *feel* like reading the Bible. And besides, I never remember what I read." Dear one, you're not training for a Bible quiz—you're *eating*. I don't remember what I ate last Thursday, but it did my body good. I may not always remember brilliant flashes of insight that light up the dark recesses of my spirit, but when I read the Scriptures, my spirit is being fed by the Holy Spirit—who is both the ever-present Comforter and the Source of the Word of God (see John 16:13).

Stand above condemnation. The Adversary would like nothing better than to keep an already burdened spirit stooped even lower with a load of condemnation. This is that depression that comes when you can't help dwelling on all the reasons you don't deserve anything good in life. The accusing whispers seem to scream, "With your past, why should God answer your prayers? Guilt and heaviness, unhappiness and problems—they are just what you deserve." Memorize 1 John 3:20-21 for such times: "If our heart condemns us, God is greater than our heart . . . if our heart does not condemn us, we have confidence toward God." John is dealing with the tension between conviction and condemnation. Conviction will draw you to Jesus; condemnation will make you tell yourself how little you deserve to be there. And of course we *don't* deserve His grace! But the next time that lying condemnation whispers, "You don't deserve God's goodness," just reply, "Right! So now I'll just praise the Lord *again!*"

Give forgiveness freely. There's nothing so wearying to the spirit as carrying around bitterness or rancor toward others. How easy it is to forget Matthew 6:12: "Forgive us our debts, *as we forgive our debtors*" (emphasis added). This means that if I insist on carrying a grudge against others, I can't expect Jesus to lift even the sense of my own burden from my soul!

As a result, I consign myself to a double load.

Offer praise amid turmoil. Let's deal with that oft-quoted passage, "In everything give thanks; for this is the will of God in Christ Jesus for you" (1 Thess. 5:18). Let's not make the mistake of thinking the Bible means that we should praise the Lord in the middle of catastrophes because such events are God's will for us. Many of our problems may well be Satan's work, not God's. But that verse does express divine wisdom. Praising God in the midst of difficulty stakes out God's territory over against Satan's. I'm sure it wasn't easy for the three Hebrew children in the book of Daniel to praise God in the midst of the fiery furnace. They were not praising the fire; rather, they were praising the presence of God with them *in* the fire. In times of difficulty, we must assert Jesus' overpowering presence by faith.

Sing about hope. Isaiah 54:1-3 tells us to sing when there is no life in the womb, and life will come forth. Not everyone has a biological womb, but everyone has a womb-shaped heart created for gestating dreams and carrying embryonic hopes. God says to "sing" over these dreams and hope, and He will bring new life from them. The song of faith builds bridges over nothingness, and God's power touches dreams and brings them to reality!

Pray continually. Finally, to sustain faith, let your problems continually find you *"continuing steadfastly in prayer"* (Rom. 12:12, emphasis added). Certainly we need regular occasions of prayer such as daily devotionals, but Paul has in mind here a constant *attitude* of prayer that we must develop in order to sustain faith in difficult times. This is the prayer breathed while we wait for the traffic signal to change; the inner hope expressed as we sit down at our desk first thing in the morning; the God-consciousness that leads us to pray, even in the middle of a heated argument, "Lord, bless my tongue!"

All of these keys to sustaining faith are related to and focused on Jesus. None is a quick fix or a magic talisman; all depend on the presence of Christ and His sovereign will. In the midst of life's fragmenting stress, remember that *"In [Christ] all things hold together"* (Col. 1:17, *NIV,* emphasis added). It is in the working of Him who holds even our lives together that these six keys to sustaining faith have the power to unlock every door Satan may slam in our faces. Hallelujah!

praise in prayer

I praise You, God of strength, for the power of Your Word, for Your indwelling Spirit, and for the gift of forgiveness. In times that call for sustained faith, dear Father, help me to praise You with honesty. Even when I am troubled, help me to sing in the darkness and to continue steadfastly in prayer. Sustain my faith, I pray, through Jesus, amen.

selected Readings

Psalm 69:13-18   Matthew 11:28-30

praise in practice

1. What do you habitually do just before retiring at night? Take a walk? Read the paper? Work a crossword puzzle? Watch a late-night television program? Each night for a week, the last thing before going to sleep, try reading a Bible passage or a devotional reading. Report on any differences

this makes in your outlook the next morning.

2. Meditate on whether you are harboring hard feelings toward anyone. Focus on the fact that God has forgiven you, and then release any hard feelings you may have toward someone else.

3. Share a situation in which prayer leaped to your lips without any formal prompting such as "Let us pray."

singing the song of God in a strange land

By the rivers of Babylon, there we sat down, yea,
we wept when we remembered Zion. We hung our harps
upon the willows in the midst of it. For . . . how shall we
sing the LORD's song in a foreign land?

PSALM 137:1-4

In my book *Taking Hold of Tomorrow,* I relate how during my childhood, when I was five years old, my family's move from southern California caused me to leave all my friends. We settled in Montana, where I entered first grade. I adjusted fairly quickly—even though being the new kid on the block is never easy. Then, about the time I was feeling that Montana was home, we moved again—this time to Oakland, California—and I had to go through the adjustment process again.

Life stabilized, and by the time I made it to the fifth grade, among my "credits" was membership in the traffic patrol—jaunty hats and sweater stripes and all! But wait! Now on the brink of sixth grade and office in student government, we moved across town. All of a sudden, my friends and status were gone. Later, after becoming a pretty fair basketball player, an injured knee ended my hopes of high school stardom.

How often life's moves and changes put us in a "strange land." But hear the psalmist, for he also understands how difficult it is to sing the Lord's song in a strange land, when things become foreign to our plans. Psalm 137 probably refers to the season of exile the kingdom of Judah experienced when many were led captive to Babylon due to Judah's disobedience. You may well identify with them, for there are enough moves, upset situations and broken families in our own world for many of us to feel muted, not really ready to sing—silenced in new surroundings.

You will recall with me how God's faithfulness enabled many exiles to later return to Jerusalem. They rebuilt the Temple, restored their family homes and worshiped again in the place they had longed to see recovered. Still, it is apparent that many of those who remained in Babylon did learn to sing the Lord's song there after all. This fact has been confirmed by archaeologists who today have found evidence of a thriving Jewish community in Babylon dating back to this period of captivity. The message is moving, for we see songs that brought *recovery* and songs that made *discovery*. From this we learn that we can raise our psalms of praise to the Lord wherever we are—not just geographically but emotionally as well.

Disappointing transitions and setbacks and strange settings can spin our plans around and set our life askew. Life doesn't always work out the way it appeared it might. But our real challenge is to not let circumstances set boundaries that seem to block our prayers and thwart our attempts to continue in the song and spirit of praise. Worship frees us from such boundaries!

We don't have to pretend. We don't have to be stoic about our feelings. We can be honest and admit that it's just easier to praise in some settings than in others. But then we can go ahead and praise the Lord anyway! We honor the God who transcends the boundaries of nations, the walls of familiar churches, the barriers of mere states of mind and the situations that disappoint us.

Sing—no matter how strange or foreign your situation. You'll find that His presence transforms the strangest place in your life into a hometown—with Him close at hand.

praise in prayer

O God, You who are everywhere present,
I praise You for being available regardless of
time and place and circumstance. Help me to be
at home in Your world, wherever I am, so that
I may be faithful in praise in season and out of
season, full or in need, near or far. Through
Christ our Lord, amen.

selected readings

Daniel 1:5-21; 3:8-18   Acts 18:5-11

praise in practice

1. Have you ever moved location, lived in a foreign country or had any other type of disruption in your life that made it difficult for you to focus on praise and worship?

2. Have you ever been so attached to a church building or a particular style of church architecture that changing to a different church created a problem?

3. In Daniel 3:8-18, how did living as captives in Babylon affect the worship of the children of Israel?

4. What indication had God given Daniel and his three friends that because they had been faithful to Him, He would be with them in Babylon (see Dan. 1:5-21)?

walking within
my house

*I will sing of mercy and justice; to You, O Lord, I will sing
praises. I will behave wisely in a perfect way. . . . I will
walk within my house with a perfect heart.*

PSALM 101:1-2

HOW desperately the Lord seeks and our land needs homes in which people behave wisely today! While we may not arrive at *perfection,* we certainly can affirm our *direction* toward sinlessness and away from sin. We can be completely committed to making our homes places of mercy and justice—places where God is pleased to dwell.

How urgently does the Lord seek heads of families who will join with Joshua in saying, "As for me and my house, we will serve the LORD" (Josh. 24:15). Someone has worded it this way: "If the home fires are burning for God, the heart-fires will never chill."

One reason that God places such importance on the family is because it is there that we reveal most clearly who we really are and whom we really serve. How would I fare today if God took a census of my home? How would you fare? Ask yourself, *What would such a census reveal about . . .*

The way I speak and act in private;

The reading material I surround myself with;

The music that fills my dwelling;

The table talk the family shares . . . or doesn't;

The forgiveness displayed to one another;

The food and beverages that characterize my lifestyle;

The money plans I have and exercise;
The magazines that fill the rack;
The moods I invite or tolerate;
The entertainment I seek and foster;
The media input I welcome via cable TV, radio,
     CDs;
The Savior I praise and worship?

The purpose of walking through this list is neither a rigid review nor an exercise in nosiness. The fact is that God *does* take such a census. The question should really be: What if He published it? The bottom line is that our behavior at home indicates *whom* we are serving— are we serving Him, ourselves, or the world system?

The call of God is to behave wisely at home, saying, "As for me and *everything in and about my house*, the *Lord will be served*. Not myself, not carnal entertainment, not fickle moods, not warring relationships, but Christ will be central, worshiped and glorified!"

Joshua made this application to the family by the attention he gave to *monuments* and *memorials*. When God accomplished a significant victory through the people, they erected a memorial—both to honor God and to remind their children of how God had worked among them (see Josh. 4:1-7; 24:24-27).

Let's never substitute the value of Sunday School or Christian schools for our own responsibility to educate our children, for we too *must* establish memorable and "monumental" moments. Children remember best what they see put into action. They need parents who are living incarnations of the Word the parents want their children to learn. Joshua's monuments demonstrate the dramatic importance of parents sharing with their children *how God's truth worked in their own experience.*

Take time to pour yourself into your children. Tell them how you were saved, how God has led and protected you, and how He continues to lead you toward the Promised Land. There is no wiser way to "walk" within your house!

praise in prayer

We praise You, God, for being our Father and for the blessings of being in Your family. Help us to live together in families of both biological and spiritual kinship in ways that glorify You. Help our private walk to indicate to those closest to us that You are our Father. Through Christ we pray, amen.

selected readings

Psalm 127   Joshua 4:1-7

praise in practice

1. Share with a group any family traditions that are like the memorials of Joshua—ways of bringing to mind the good things God has done.

2. Discuss any stresses in family life that challenge attempts to place Christ at the center. For example, have you been able to have family devotionals? Do society's demands (work, school, peer pressure and so on) make it more difficult to place Christ at the center of your life?

You can sleep because God doesn't

I will both lie down in peace, and sleep; for You alone, O LORD, make me dwell in safety.

PSALM 4:8

The Lord often awakens me during the night. Someone may suspect that it's indigestion or worry, but I've learned to tell the difference between times of sleeplessness and those times when the Lord calls, wanting to impress something on my mind. Not long ago I was awakened in this way, and I went to the place in our living room where I usually go for my devotions. I wondered what it was He wanted to say to me.

I had been unusually laden with duty, with much on my mind, and so I shouldn't have been surprised. But it was so tender a message, simply "Everything's going to be all right. Now, back to bed and sleep." And I did just that. Even though no *conscious* turmoil had awakened me, a full plate of duty had induced a mental "indigestion" that needed the Father's assuring word of comfort—the comfort of His personal interest and promise of provision.

The psalmist says, "He who keeps you will not slumber. Behold, He who keeps Israel shall neither slumber nor sleep" (Ps. 121:3-4). It's a part of the supernatural nature of God that He isn't subject to the weariness of body and spirit that makes sleep essential for human beings. One is reminded of the simple words reportedly spoken by Pope John XXIII upon retiring nightly: "I go to sleep, Lord. The Church is Yours."

It's hard to imagine, but apparently after we have been ushered into God's divine presence in heaven, we won't need sleep either. John's report of his vision of the New Jerusalem states, "There shall be no night there: They need no lamp nor light of the sun, for the Lord God gives them light" (Rev. 22:5). If we sleep in heaven, apparently we'll have to learn to do it in the daytime!

In any case, in this life we *do* need our sleep. Worry and depression and life's hectic pace can make getting the sleep we need problematic. Car trouble, a business reversal, a problem in personal or family relationships, difficulty on the job—any of a thousand other things—can interfere with our sleep. Like a thief, sleeplessness can creep into our minds under cover of night's dark shades, robbing us of the sleep we need.

When it happens, declare this firm promise: Sleep is ours, a gift from the Creator of night and day, who promises that we can both lie down in peace and sleep. Make your last thought at night that God is up, well, and remaining watchful over you and all that concerns you. Leave things to Him. He can get more done on your problem while you're asleep than you can while you're awake!

praise in prayer

You created me to sleep, dear Lord, and You know how much I need. Just as I need physical rest, provide rest for my soul in the assurance of Your constant care and watchfulness. And when I need to be awake, open my eyes and ears—alert me to Your voice and Your will. I trust myself to You, O Father, the Lord of both my nights and my days, amen.

selected readings

1 Kings 18:20-29   Ecclesiastes 8:16-17

praise in practice

1. Do your sleeping habits reflect worry? Depression? What do you do when you can't sleep?

2. Write up a little scene that illustrates the fact that God doesn't sleep but is in charge of the world even through the darkest night—situations that convey His care for you. For example, imagine that you're a king and that you have a trusted guard posted at the castle door. Be creative as you write this brief scene. Read this bedtime story to yourself just before going to sleep at night.

3. Do some people sleep too much? Have you known this to be the case with yourself or with someone you love (see Prov. 6:1-11)?

DAY 30

i want somebody to know my name

*O LORD, You have searched me and known me. You know
my sitting down and my rising up; You understand my
thought afar off. You comprehend my path and my lying
down, and are acquainted with all my ways.*

PSALM 139:1-3

CATHY MEEKS WAS A YOUNG AFRICAN AMERICAN engaged in the civil rights struggle during the racial unrest of the 1960s. She was raised a Christian and sought to respect authority, so at first she was hesitant to take to the streets to demonstrate against injustice. But with the shooting of a black child in the Los Angeles suburb of Watts, something inside her broke. She felt the circumstance demanded that she join the protest—so Cathy marched.

However, Cathy still felt that she was caught between surging waves of humanity. On the one hand were the defenders of the status quo; she knew they were not as just as they should be. On the other hand were the protest leaders, in whom she often sensed a rebellious spirit—a spirit that she felt wasn't in harmony with her Christian upbringing. She asked herself where she belonged, a question that raised deeper questions of who she was, down deep, and whether anyone really cared. Out of her agony, Cathy Meeks wrote the moving book of her experiences titled *I Want Somebody to Know My Name*.

Do you ever feel the same longing? Especially when you are torn between issues, do you wonder where God is? At such times, we all need the reassurance that we aren't lost in space, drifting among the stars, alone and unknown in the cosmos. And that's exactly what this text addresses so eloquently. Praise the Lord, in declaring this inspired statement, David offers us just that kind of reassurance. In Psalm 139, he affirms how surely our God is not merely an impersonal force in a mechanical universe. The Lord is described as being on such intimate terms with us that He is acquainted with all our ways. He is not only the God of John 3:16 who loves *the world,* He is also the God of Galatians 2:20 "who loved *me* and gave Himself for *me*" (emphasis added).

What a matter for praise! Here is the eternal God whose almighty Word keeps spinning galaxies and worlds from falling out of orbit as they continue their trek through the vastness of space, yet He tended to my prenatal development (see Ps. 139:13-16) and knows the number of the hairs on my head (see Matt. 10:30). The God who oversees the governments of the world and who limits the boundaries of the seas has stooped to be my personal Shepherd (see Ps. 23). He tracks the path of every soul ever born, and He knows me, you—and each one of His countless sheep—*by name* (see John 10:3).

The desire to be known is more than a shallow quest for notoriety, like fame seekers who lust to see their names in lights or headlines. Rather, this quest is welcomed by our Father who calls us to Himself. Let your desire—indeed, hunger—for One to know your name drive you to worship at the feet of the God who not only knows you well, but who also *loves* you and, wonder of wonders, who welcomes you to know Him!

praise in prayer

I worship You, O my God, as Sovereign over the vastness of the universe, who alone has the whole world in His hand. I praise You also as my personal Lord, who knows me by name, even better than I know myself. Thank You for Your nearness and Your unfailing love for me—personally. In the name of Jesus, my Lord, amen.

selected readings

1 Samuel 3:1-9   Psalm 8

praise in practice

1. Take a flashlight and a Bible outdoors one night—preferably in a quiet place when the stars are out. Stand quietly for a few moments looking up at the sky. Breathe deeply. Try to imagine how far you're looking and ponder the vastness of the universe. Now use your flashlight to find and read 1 Kings 19:11-13. Ask yourself God's question to Elijah: "What are you doing here?" Is it difficult to imagine that in all this vastness God sees you and knows you?

2. Discuss with friends any feelings of loneliness you may have, or the feeling that no one knows the real you.

His kingdom is now!

Your saints shall bless You. They shall speak of the glory of Your kingdom, and talk of Your power, to make known to the sons of men His mighty acts, and the glorious majesty of His kingdom.

PSALM 145:10-12

sometimes we long so fervently for the coming of the kingdom at the last great day that we forget that the kingdom of God, in power and glory, is available *now* to those who worship His Majesty, Jesus Christ. Our Savior ascended the throne as the majestic Son of David when He was raised from the dead (see Acts 2:30). He commissioned His followers to make disciples among the nations by the authority and power of that throne (see Matt. 28:18-20). The apostle Paul said that those who had responded to this invitation had been "conveyed . . . into the kingdom of the Son of His love" (Col. 1:13). God's kingdom is *now!*

This takes nothing away from the fact that the Kingdom will not be realized in its fullness until Jesus returns in clouds of glory. But it is to impress upon us the glorious fact that we have access *now*, by faith, to the power of the King if we live and worship as citizens of His kingdom. One of Satan's most insidious tactics is to make us look with dismay at the smaller battles he wins around us every day, forgetting that our King has already won the greatest battle—that the final revelation of His victory only awaits His chosen moment. Regardless of how bleak the circumstances may seem or how shadowed the horizons may appear by reason of the Adversary's desperate and despicable tactics, the fact remains that Jesus has bequeathed to us a life of power and of triumph in the resources of His kingdom. *Everything God has promised to us already exists. All that remains for us to do is walk with Him until we come to the place where each fulfilled promise is waiting.*

So as we walk and wait, let us worship His majesty.

Majesty, worship His majesty,
Unto Jesus be all glory, honor and praise.
Majesty, kingdom authority,
Flows from His throne unto His own,
    His anthem raise.
So exalt, lift up on high
    the name of Jesus.
Magnify, come glorify,
Christ Jesus the king.
Majesty, worship His majesty,
Jesus who died, now glorified,
    King of all kings.[1]

praise in prayer

King of kings and Lord of lords, I praise You in Your majesty, acknowledging Your power over all evil, doubt and fear that would rob me of victory. In Your name and by Your authority, I pronounce Satan and his forces to be vanquished. I bow before You, my Lord and King, and glorify the Father, by the power of Your Spirit, according to Your Word and in Your matchless name! Amen.

Note

1. Jack Hayford, "Worship His Majesty," © 1981 Rocksmith Music. All rights reserved.

suggestions for your daily devotions

Are you looking for a simple yet effective way to invite God into your life? Many people feel this need but have difficulty moving from a vague feeling to taking the concrete steps upward to the Throne and into His presence. Here are a few suggestions.[1]

For private devotions, and in some family settings, there's nothing like asking God first thing in the morning to order your day. As the psalmist said, "My voice You shall hear in the morning, O LORD; in the morning I will direct it to You" (Ps. 5:3). We don't call it "daybreak" for nothing; for in God's presence the day can be . . .

- Broken open like a *gift*, surprising our hearts with His provision.
- Broken open like an *egg*, with life bursting forth as simply and brightly as a yellow chick.
- Broken open like the *sky*, with shafts of light splitting dewdrops into rainbows of promise.

Every day, there are new worlds to be won through the newness that happens when we begin the day by walking with Jesus, making our steps fit into His

- in prayer,
- in the Word, and
- in faithful response to His love.

Whether it's at daybreak or day's end, over that midmorning cup of coffee with a Christian neighbor or friend, at the office during the noon break, or in a group or in privacy, here is a pattern of devotion that has been helpful to many.

1. Begin with *thanksgiving* and *praise*, simply verbalizing to God how you experience His majesty. Like aerobics, this heart-expanding experience will increase your capacity to receive more and more of Him every day.

2. Move into *confession*. Dare to name your shortcomings, facing them down in the holy name of Jesus. But don't wallow in them as though you didn't trust the blood that cleanses us from all sin! Instead, joyfully accept the forgiveness Christ offers.

3. Have a *Bible reading* and/or a brief reading such as those in this book. Allow the Word to set a theme and tone to remember. If there is time and you are in a group, focus

your awareness of the theme through discussions and exercises such as the "Praise in Practice" sections in this book.

4. *Intercede* for family and friends, your church and community, nations and their leaders. Pray in specifics, trusting that the fervent prayer of righteous people "avails much" (Jas. 5:16).

5. *Submit* to the Father in prayer. It's good to kneel or raise your hands if possible to allow your body to approve what your spirit is pledging: your willingness to live in obedience to His loving but kingly rule. A brief closing prayer is also provided at the end of each of this book's daily devotionals.

I pray that the Scriptures, the comments and the prayers in this book will open for you new and fresh vistas on the power of praise. May the time you spend with this material glorify God through His Son and enrich your everyday walk.

Note

1. These suggestions are adapted from *Daybreak* by Jack Hayford (Wheaton, IL: Tyndale House, 1987).